100 Teaching Ideas that Transfer and Transform Learning

Expand your teaching repertoire with this unique collection of instructional ideas. Author Frank T. Lyman Jr., esteemed educator and creator of the Think-Pair-Share model, offers ways to help students think critically, encounter puzzling phenomena and seek explanations, think before responding, listen to responses from others, create their own questions, visualize a scene, employ problem-solving strategies, and more.

Appropriate for teachers of all grades and subjects, the ideas address the pursuit of true learning—wanting to learn, how to learn, and enabling to learn—and can easily be adapted and applied to a wide variety of contexts.

The book's format allows you to pick and choose activities for your own professional development journey and make them your own, so you can expand your teaching toolbox and bring more students to deeper levels of learning.

Frank T. Lyman Jr. is an award-winning educator and author. He was an elementary school teacher in Massachusetts and Maryland and a field-based University of Maryland, College Park Teacher Education Center Coordinator for both university students and classroom teachers. He discovered and collaborated in the development of teaching strategies such as Think-Pair-Share, cognitive mapping, and the ThinkTrix. His recognitions include the National Association of Teacher Educators Clinician of the Year, the University of Maryland Presidential Award for Outstanding Service to the Schools, and the University of Maryland College of Education Alumni Association Outstanding Professional Award.

100 Teaching Ideas that Transfer and Transform Learning

Expanding your Repertoire

Frank T. Lyman Jr.

Routledge
Taylor & Francis Group

NEW YORK AND LONDON

First published 2022
by Routledge
605 Third Avenue, New York, NY 10158

and by Routledge
2 Park Square, Milton Park, Abingdon, Oxon, OX14 4RN

Routledge is an imprint of the Taylor & Francis Group, an informa business

Library of Congress Cataloging-in-Publication Data
A catalog record for this book has been requested

ISBN: 978-1-032-13645-5 (hbk)
ISBN: 978-1-032-12664-7 (pbk)
ISBN: 978-1-003-23028-1 (ebk)

DOI: 10.4324/9781003230281

Typeset in Palatino
by Apex CoVantage, LLC

This book is dedicated to the memory of and in admiration of Bill Ferguson, a University of Maryland graduate, who, for ten years despite serious illness, with every fiber of his high intellect, skill, and love of children exemplified what it is to be a great teacher.

Contents

Preface

Ideas count. They are hard-won through experience in teaching. In the form of concepts, hypotheses, propositions, or principles they can be applied in multiple situations. In other words, they can be transferred to other challenges. Because they have multiple applications, they can be more practical than a good lesson plan that is only used once.

This book is a compendium of activities, strategies, and techniques within which are ideas that can be applied in many contexts. The more applications a given idea has, the more positive effect it will have on teaching/learning situations. For instance, within the **Think-Pair-Share** technique are at least two widely applicable principles—individual think time, or Wait Time, and pair response. Every classroom discussion should allow students to think, or rehearse, before they are asked to respond, and students responding to each other in pairs has multiple learning and social values. **Think-Pair-Share** is an elegant incorporation of these two principles, but they can transfer to use with other activities and variations as Think-Pair-Share itself can.

All the suggestions in this book are embedded with general principles. To use the book to expand repertoire, the reader is advised to think of the principle(s) embedded in the suggestion and how they could be applied in multiple contexts. For instance, there are several suggestions in the book that feature the importance of teacher-student relationships and give ways to enhance them. The principle is that the more a student feels noticed and cared about by a teacher, the more responsive the student will be to the learning opportunities presented. The best use of this book is to glean the underlying principles of the suggestion and to think about where they can be applied in different ways. This is a thinking teacher's book, a source of ideas that can transfer, that can in effect "travel" to other situations. No amount of lesson plan suggestions or advice from a supervisor can match the effectiveness and repertoire building of a teacher who knows how to learn through the transfer of ideas to future practice. Through (or by) looking for connections and spin-offs of powerful ideas, teachers become their own professional developers.

View this book as having usable activities and embedded ideas that will help create teaching and learning as a personal adventure. Open to any page.

Propositions From This Book

Following are some sample propositions from activities in the book. When tested they may become principles that are generally applicable in other areas or circumstances. Find and test your own and be your own professional developer.

Students who have time to think before responding will be more interested in the responses of others.

Students who encounter puzzling phenomena will seek explanations.

Students who are read to will be more interested in reading themselves.

Students who learn about something deeply will be more likely to want to do so again.

Students who feel noticed by the teacher will be more willing to learn.

Students who know the basic thinking types will create questions, consciously.

Students who discuss content in pairs will remember the content more completely.

Students who visualize a scene will create more precise descriptions.

Students who have learned by multiple examples will be better able to define a concept or generalize.

Students who learn a problem-solving strategy will be more able to analyze and solve problems.

Students who recreate scenes in writing will become better story writers.

Students who induce their own grammar rules will be more likely to adhere to them in their writing.

Meet the Author

Frank T. Lyman Jr. was an elementary school teacher in Massachusetts and Maryland from 1960 to 1970, and a field-based University of Maryland, College Park, Teacher Education Center coordinator for both university students and classroom teachers, K–12, in Howard County, Maryland, from 1970 to 1996. He discovered and collaborated on the development of teaching strategies such as Think-Pair-Share, cognitive mapping, and the ThinkTrix. He worked with teachers, student teachers, graduate students, and university colleagues to develop reflective teacher tools, such as theory-practice templates and a problem-solving/research design. He is a graduate of St. Albans School, Haverford College, the Harvard Graduate School of Education, and the University of Maryland, College Park. His doctoral dissertation at Maryland [1978] focused on teachers' significant and durable learning experiences.

Since 1996, he has taught courses on pedagogy and leadership and consulted in the areas of critical thinking for students and educational leaders. His recognitions include the National Association of Teacher Educators Clinician of the Year, 1989; the University of Maryland Presidential Award for Outstanding Service to the Schools, 1996; and the University of Maryland College of Education Alumni Association Outstanding Professional Award of 2010. His publications related to this book are *The Shaping of Thought: A Teacher's Guide to Metacognitive Mapping and Critical Thinking in Response to Literature* with Charlene Lopez and Arlene Mindus, Rowman and Littlefield, 2017, and *ThinkTrix: Tools to Teach 7 Essential Thinking Skills*, Kagan Publishing, 2016.

Acknowledgments

The strategies, techniques, and epiphanies that accumulate and make up a teacher's repertoire arise through a synergy among colleagues and with students. Over 600 teachers, student teachers, graduate students, administrators, professors, researchers, field-based teacher educators, and professional developers are some of those who are connected to the 100 entries in this book. They are codevelopers, implementers, inventors, and encouragers, without whom many of the ideas would not have existed in the form presented. The 600 and others know who they are, and 15 are mentioned here for their importance to some central concerns of the book and its production. They are **Arlene Mindus**, a master cooperating teacher and principal who is a coinventor of Think-Pair-Share and the ThinkTrix typology; **Charlene Lopez**, a master teacher in language arts and a coinventor of the ThinkTrix typology; **Shirley Rogers**, who for 43 years teaching at all developmental levels used and developed many of the ideas in the book; **Spencer Kagan**, who spread Think-Pair-Share around the world and recognized through publication the paradigm shift within the ThinkTrix strategy; **Neil Davidson** whose devotion to cooperative learning facilitated a national movement; **Jay McTighe**, for his ongoing support of key ideas in this book and relentless pursuit of the Big Ideas and transfer; **Richard Arends** for his expertise in teacher education and ongoing support and advice on the book; **George Eley**, a Maryland University professor whose dedication to beginning teachers resulted in a game-changing way to problem solve; **Lynda Tredway**, whose work with administrators toward reflection, research, and expanding the learning space for all students inspires the author; **John Strebe**, the Johnny Appleseed of Think-Pair-Share and original cooperative learning strategies for secondary math; **Francis Baranson**, a 43-year middle school science teacher who made curiosity motivation central; **Chips Merkle**, a special education teacher whose success with Think-Pair-Share and ThinkTrix with language-challenged children seemed miraculous; **Thomas Brown**, an elementary school principal who practiced and promoted innovative teaching for minority students; **Thommie DePinto Piercy**, whose work with metacognition and cognitive mapping ("metamapping") was a model for Maryland teachers; and **Pete Bielski**, a superb field-based teacher educator who conceived of this book with the author.

It seems appropriate to mention some of the places of origin of the content, in that place and opportunity play a role in educational improvement. These are at least Haverford College; the field-heavy Harvard Graduate School of Education master's program in the 1960s; Somerset Elementary School in Montgomery County, Maryland; the Estabrook School in Lexington Massachusetts, where the Harvard/Lexington Ford Foundation team teaching project took place in 1961–1970; Bowman Elementary in Lexington; the Harvard/Newton master's program for interns; the Howard County Schools in Maryland; the staff development departments in most Maryland Counties; the University of Maryland, College Park, field-based master's and doctoral programs; the Reading Center at the University of Maryland; and most remarkable and long-lasting of all, the learning environments in the national award-winning University of Maryland, College Park/Maryland public schools Teacher Education Centers for undergraduate and graduate student teachers from 1967 to 1996, K–12. The public schools and the university became extensions of each other with jointly appointed field coordinators as catalysts for the invention of ameliorative responses to the nagging problems of classroom teaching and learning. Some of the results of this relatively seamless collaboration are entries in this book.

I would also like to thank my daughter Sarah Lyman Kravits for her support and expertise in the preparation of the manuscript. Finally, I am indebted to my editor, Lauren Davis, for believing in the concept of the book and carrying it through to publication. Her belief in this work enhances my own.

Section I

Learning to Learn—the Student as Aware and Persevering Thinker

Two keys to learning are knowing how to learn and being motivated to do so. This section focuses on learning how to learn and on motivation. When students understand and strategically employ learning strategies, the independence and the motivation that result will make it more likely that they persevere as lifelong learners. The activities and ideas in this section are designed to help toward this end.

The question to be answered is: *How can students learn how to learn on their own and be motivated to do so?*

DOI: 10.4324/9781003230281-1

1

Inspire to Inquire

What is the fuel of learning if not curiosity? The intrinsic desire to know something is essential to true education, both short term and lifelong. The best stimulator of curiosity is a problematic or incongruous fact, situation, or idea. These motivators can be the beginning and center of every unit, lesson, or class day. (See Appendix Figure A.1, **Classroom Motivation Wheel**.) Teachers as well as students can find the weirdest facts about any subject and see where they lead. The facts can "ambush" the students' minds. Discrepancy pursued leads to congruency. True learning is pursuit. "In any field, find the strangest thing and explore it" was said by John Wheeler, the man who proved black holes exist (quoted in James Gleick, *Genius: The Life and Science of Richard Feynman*, 1993).

Education Should Be an Itch Before a Scratch

DOI: 10.4324/9781003230281-2

2

Connectors of the Mind

Schema theory holds that knowledge is interconnected in the mind in a design. This being true, the interconnections, or nodes, of this network are of interest to the teacher. Though the content of each person's knowledge schema is different, some interconnecting points can be held in common. What might these be and how might they be taught? In general terms, the nodes in a network of knowledge vary in nature and are specific to the category. They are concepts, facts, events, generalizations, attitudes, strategies, or skills: in math—properties, theorems, patterns, formulas, problem-solving strategies; in language—words, quotes, genres, skills, themes; in social studies—events, people, facts, case studies, concepts, generalizations; in science—experiments, hypotheses, theories, phenomena; in the arts—styles, genres, skills, people, media. Each of these knowledge connectors is a place to which the learners can return to remember, expand, adjust, and use knowledge. They are connectors that will not always stay the same, changing in accuracy and importance as the individual's schema develops. The teacher's role is to help shape this development by recognizing the structural nature of knowledge, making available some of the connectors, teaching the students how to use them, and emphasizing the **Big Ideas**, a term popularized by Jay McTighe (see Glossary).

The Real Internet

DOI: 10.4324/9781003230281-3

3

Enfranchise Student Minds

For some students a teacher may appear to be a high priest of the mind, asking runic questions and giving cryptic tasks, such as, "What do you think about this story?" or, "Analyze this problem." Besides translating such questions and tasks, the teacher can demystify the classroom discourse by teaching students how their minds work. Fundamental thinking types, or "mind actions," can be learned by students in grades 1–12. As codified by the ThinkTrix, a thinking matrix typology, could be *recall*, *similarity*, *difference*, *cause and effect*, *example to idea*, *idea to example*, and *evaluation* (see Figures A.11-13). Once students understand and can manipulate these basic mind actions, they are able to construct questions at varied levels, translate thinking in texts and tests, translate teacher and peer questions, and create test questions for themselves. When this understanding is established through multiple examples, students are able to answer for themselves the question: "How should my mind work to answer this question or solve this problem?" They are now metacognitive and can act consciously to find the answer.

Awareness Frees the Mind

DOI: 10.4324/9781003230281-4

4

Teach Them Metacognition

A teacher's goal is to help create critical thinkers and independent learners. One mark of effective teaching is the extent to which students want to and are able to learn after the lesson, unit, or school year. Student perseverance is a hallmark of teaching excellence. Beyond the necessity of intrinsic motivation, or the drive to know, is the equally important element of learning strategy, or <u>how</u> to know. Students need to know the thinking paths to problem-solving, decision-making, inquiring, and creating, as well as the mind actions, or thinking types, required along these paths. Intellectual independence rests upon meta knowledge or knowing about knowing. They should learn to use their minds as a carpenter uses tools—skillfully and strategically. Some basic "tools" are **recall**, **similarity**, **difference**, **cause and effect**, **idea to example**, **example to idea**, and **evaluation** (see **thinking types** in Glossary).

Fishing for a Lifetime

DOI: 10.4324/9781003230281-5

5

A Cognitive Path to Solutions

Problem-solving is life's crucial process. Though this fact is generally acknowledged to be true, most suggestions for steps in problem-solving leave out the examining of causes. Words like *analysis*, *understanding the problem*, and *mess finding* are presented to students as steps toward a solution. None of these prompts tell students precisely how their minds should work to proceed. Another flaw in many problem-solving paths is that the way to define a problem is stated simply as "define the problem." What a defined problem looks like is not made clear. These two steps and others are easily clarified by using precise language. The process in several steps can be flow charted out in the following way:

♦ State the problem cleanly without any reference to causes.
♦ State the effects of the problem. Is the problem worth solving?
♦ List all the possible causes of the problem. Are there hidden causes?
♦ Decide which cause[s] are the most important or weighted.
♦ Choose some of the causes to mitigate or eradicate.
♦ Design a solution that is directly related to the key causes.

DOI: 10.4324/9781003230281-6

- ♦ Think through the possible positive and negative effects of this solution.
- ♦ Redesign the solution if necessary.
- ♦ Try the solution and note the positive or negative effects.
- ♦ If necessary, rethink the entire process.
- ♦ If it worked, ask what can be learned by the success.
- ♦ Throughout the process ask what other situation or problem is similar.

See sample flowcharts in Appendix Figures A.2–A.5.

Flowchart It, Practice It, Let Them Do It

6

Linking the Thinking

Picture a classroom in which students are thinking about the content diagrammatically. Choosing from a repertoire of about 30 visual organizers/ThinkLinks or creating their own shapes, they are connecting ideas to examples, causes to effects, one case by analogy to another (see some in Appendix Figures A.6 and A.7). They are working individually, in pairs, or in cooperative groups of four. After completing the Think Link, they label the types of thinking they used, then sometimes proceed to use the completed maps as blueprints for discussion or written composition.

All Thought Has Shape

DOI: 10.4324/9781003230281-7

7

Student Experts

Being an expert at some skill or an expert in some body of knowledge is highly motivating. Some colleges and graduate schools make this premise the center of their programs. Younger students are no less capable of doing something well or knowing deeply. A suggestion would be to begin a school year with the requirement that each student over time find an area of interest and learn about it. This would entail reading, note taking, and where possible using the internet. Black holes, a civil war battle, a president, Greek words in English, a famous painter, famous people, poetry, urban life, economics, chess, American Revolution, a sport, causes of war, climate change, famous discoveries, math anomalies, a work of art, a musical genre, essay writing, geology, an animal, plant growing, roller coaster engineering, cell biology, and countless other areas for investigation are possibilities for student "experts."

At intervals or at the end of the year, students could try to involve others in their specialty during "festivals" in which students could rotate from booth to booth to ask questions and learn from each other. Curiosity is the fuel of education, and curiosity plus relevance to the learner is high octane. This opportunity to learn something in-depth is likely to spill over into other classroom activities. Student attitude is at stake here. Further, when expert level is reached, the information or skill becomes a

DOI: 10.4324/9781003230281-8

powerful node in a network of knowledge, which Jerome Bruner called a "structure of knowledge."[1] From this node, by analogy, much more can and will be learned, both about content and about how to learn on one's own.

Interest at the Heart of Expertise

Note

1. From *The Process of Education,* Jerome Bruner, Vintage Books, 1963

8

Students as Knowledge Makers

How do people learn? What makes a great teacher? Why use Wait Time? What causes conflicts? What causes prejudice? What are the effects of prejudice? Why do people fake? What are the causes and effects of bullying? How can conflicts be resolved? How does a scientist find the hypothesis? How are friendships formed? What is beautiful about mathematics? What makes great art? These questions and many more that students could craft form a treasure chest for inquiry. Responding to them can lead to the **Big Ideas**.[1]

The most important aspect of students trying to answer "essential questions" is that they can do much of it cooperatively from their prior knowledge. Once having created a cluster of responses and further questions around the questions, students will see themselves as knowledge makers, not simply as consumers. To the extent that their minds are in this way enfranchised, they will be more likely to be lifetime learners, in the same manner that students who do original writing may continue to believe in themselves as writers.

An effective strategy for uncovering the students' knowledge toward a hypothesis or a theory is first to have each student brainstorm all the possible causes, effects, analogies, or elements related to the question. The teacher models the use of familiar

DOI: 10.4324/9781003230281-9

and relevant contexts from which to derive the common causes, effects, or analogies. Stressing that the answer will be a corporate achievement, the teacher then has the students work in pairs to discuss and add to what they wrote individually. The pairs then go to squares and all the knowledge is afterward shared with the teacher and collected on a concentric ring circular visual organizer (see Appendix Figure A.8). After the teacher sculptures out, or combines, the overlapping concepts, the students' work can be placed accessibly for reference. Done frequently, this activity could improve all the students' attitudes about their efficacy as learners. After all, students persisting as interested and confident learners is the true mark of great teaching. Persistence and confidence can be achieved through a constructivist approach in the classroom.

Construct It; Own It

Note

1.   From *Teaching For Deeper Learning:* Tools to Engage Students in Making Meaning, Jay McTighe and Harvey Silver, ASCD, 2020

9

Decisions—Rationales and Consequences

Decisions crowd everyone's day. No one is immune from having to make decisions, so how should education deal with this reality? The answer may lie in the study of decisions themselves. What factors influence them? How are consequences predetermined? How are unintended consequences dealt with? When are they reversed? What are the most important ones faced by students? What are the most important ones in our world, in world and national history?

To move to a general understanding of the key elements in decision-making, the teacher can challenge and enable students to become experts in decisions related to the content being studied or in other contexts. How was it decided that doctors should wash their hands? How did a certain artist decide to take an artistic path? How did the teacher decide to become a teacher? How was the decision made for the United States to go to war in 1812? How was it decided to "throw" the Boston Tea Party? Why did a certain famous scientist or mathematician decide to become one? What influenced a certain writer to write? Why did a talented athlete decide on one sport over another? How does a catcher decide what pitch the pitcher should throw? And what were the

DOI: 10.4324/9781003230281-10

consequences of all these decisions? Students could interview their parents or other adults as their subjects. History, public affairs, the disciplines, sports, and the arts are perfect sources for investigation into the decision-making process. From the sharing in pairs and small groups of the results of the "experts' " inquiries, the teacher and class can derive a set of general considerations influencing decision-making. Once these general discoveries are charted visually, students can analyze their own decision-making processes in their light. (See Appendix Figure A.9.) Asking them to tell what they will take from this experience into their daily living may enable the transfer of what they have learned.

Should I?

10

Ask Me a Question

When working one-on-one with a student, a teacher can become frustrated by giving an apparently clear explanation and leaving the student still perplexed. Since an objective in education is to enfranchise the minds of students to take ownership of their learning, a useful individual coaching strategy is for the teacher at times to respond only when the student asks a question. This works particularly well in math when students may miss part of the teacher's explanation as they try to process through the stress of not understanding. The teacher can model the student question process with a student, labeling it in some manner such as "student first." After the process and the rationale for it is understood, the teacher can implement it during individual conferencing on difficult math problems.

The approach can also work with group instruction but more effectively if the students write the questions down before they ask them in front of the group. The teacher can decide when to use the strategy, cueing the student(s) with "student first" when it is in place. When positive results are determined and reinforced, students can use the strategy to tutor each other. The added advantage to this latter stage is that student language is sometimes easier for students to understand. All content areas fit the strategy, and with the frequent use of their written questions,

DOI: 10.4324/9781003230281-11

students may come to see that their inquisitiveness is a necessary ingredient to learning. It is also possible that people attend best in most circumstances when the question is their own.

Students First

11

Mind Hopping

Once students have had a taste of what it feels like to write something that others can appreciate, an issue for the teacher is how to help them remember what to write about. The axiom "write what you know" is helpful only to the extent that students can access what they know and care about. One strategy they can learn is "mind hopping," or a facile moving from place to place, event to event, person to person, or time to time in the mind, thereby conjuring up memories. The teacher can effectively demonstrate this by free-associating for the class. Not only will they easily learn the strategy through this modeling, but they will also at the same time learn more about their teacher. Who is that teacher up there, and who are these classmates, and by the way, who am I? These are unspoken questions. To the degree that they are answered, the classroom can become more of a community of learners. Mind hopping, or free-associating life's experience, can be a private matter for students, preparing them to write scenes and anecdotes, or the content can be shared with a partner or larger group. The memories can then be expanded orally and put into writing, or immediately recreated in writing. The possibilities also exist for poetry, sketch writing, improvisation, and even short stories.

Memories of Things Past

DOI: 10.4324/9781003230281-12

12

The Learning Theory Lab

Telling students how they learn will not stand up in efficacy to letting them discover how they learn. This assertion can be tested when a classroom is turned into a laboratory where data can be accumulated and confirmed regarding how people learn (see Appendix Figure A.10). The "student as knowledge maker" principle is perhaps a fresher handle than student as constructivist, but the meaning is the same. For instance, recent research has shown that students fail to use study strategies that would work better in favor of long-term memory failures such as reading the information over and over. Could it be that though they have been told how to study more effectively they rejected the advice, not having had the opportunity to discover the method on their own scientifically?

The teacher can establish the classroom as a laboratory for discovering ways to learn. For instance, rereading material can be compared to visually organizing it, to repeating it to a partner, to testing each other, to making up tests for each other. Expository writing using whole models can be compared to that done from outlines. Classroom participation with Wait Time can be compared to that without time to think (refer to Appendix Figure A.8 again). Spelling without visualizing can be compared to that with visualizing. Recall of material processed individually can

DOI: 10.4324/9781003230281-13

be compared to that with cooperative processing. Vocabulary/ concepts learned through multiple contexts/examples can be compared to those learned by one example or through a definition. Spaced studying, or frequent rehearsal, can be compared to cramming, looking at long-term recall. The possibilities are endless.

A way to begin this process is to have students mine their own experience of learning in and out of school to come up with a set of hypothetical factors to be tested. This can be done in Think-Pair-Share, Think-Pair-Square fashion to achieve consensus and the factors placed on a visual organizer for all to see. Students can then design their own experiments to confirm the learning factors. Posted classroom action research on learning can turn the tables so that students take charge of their learning and no longer work against their long-term learning interests in school and as they "study" at home.

Discover the Advantage

13

Work on Attitude

Are some students afraid to do poorly in front of other students? Or is it that they fear appearing to do well in school? Along with these apparently opposite but paralyzing fears are other barriers to achievement such as fear of making errors/seeking perfection; working only for grades; fear that high expectations are unwarranted, as can occur with the "gifted" label; doing only the minimum; letting others do the thinking; and cheating. When these behaviors and their accompanying attitudes become predominant, the achievement kingdom goes to sleep. (Who will wake the princess?) To prevent or remediate counterproductive dispositions at least two approaches (princes?) are necessary: improve classroom instruction by including all students, and identify—and with the students bring to a conscious level—the offending attitudes and habits of mind and effort, complete with their causes and effects. Then teach them to be conscious of and practice the productive counterparts. Good teaching will feed on good attitudes and vice versa. Students, to win the battle with themselves, must know the enemy, and the enemy must not be allowed to flourish in school.

Disposition Is Destiny

DOI: 10.4324/9781003230281-14

14

The Seemly Side

Can beauty be taught? Can truth? Probably not, but the desire for truth and beauty can be increased in school. Aesthetic appreciation and the drive to know the truth are related, at least in the mind of the poet Keats who wrote, "Beauty is truth, truth beauty—That is all/ Ye know on earth, and all ye need to know." The path to beauty and truth is followed best and most fervently by those students who are in a state of awe.

Creating an environment where a sense of wonder can flourish is possible if the teacher believes that with curiosity, admiration, emotional response, relevance, and awe every dimension of education will be enhanced. Such a classroom might include: prints from world art; a music station with classical/popular music from all eras (Simon and Garfunkel, Mozart, Gershwin); pictures from nature; a suggestion of websites to explore (Hubble telescope pictures; deep-sea photography); mathematical formulas and puzzling problems; geometric designs; puzzles to solve; short pieces of writing, parallel translations into several languages; letters from famous people; biographies; a collection of incongruous, or discrepant, events, facts, and phenomena; great discoveries; lists and books of great literature; poetry anthologies; amazing sports stories; animal friendships; stories of cross-cultural heroism; stories of great achievements of children;

DOI: 10.4324/9781003230281-15

culturally relevant art, music, and stories; survival stories. Such stimuli and the contemplation of them will create an atmosphere in which students are motivated to learn the "basics," as well as more about the world around them and themselves. All year they can add to the collection. In June, they will leave as students for life—more able to seek, find, and appreciate what is true and what is beautiful.

"Therefore, Ye Soft Pipes, Play On."[1]

Note

1. From *Ode on a Grecian Urn* by John Keats, 1819.

15

Habits of Mind and Conscience

As promoted by Art Costa and others, productive habits of mind are core ingredients for success in school and life.[1] The question is how can teachers instill and support habits such as persistence, striving for accuracy, questioning, responding with wonder, listening with understanding and empathy, managing impulsivity, thinking flexibly, and others? One approach is for the students to construct a set of habits from their previous knowledge and personal experience and then to wall cue the concepts prominently for reference. To develop this list, the teacher and students create a pool of success stories from which they can derive the causal factors that led to the successes. The stories can be from fiction, nonfiction, and life. Through cooperative learning small groups, the teacher and students then select the most common factors leading to academic and life success. The student discoveries can be matched to the habits of mind suggested by educators. Since empathy, for instance, is a necessary habit of good character and an attribute of a civilized conscience, students can also be shown to see it and other social habits as attributes of civil character that they can then display along with the habits of mind.

In using this constructivism approach, the teacher can achieve student ownership, build a system of reminders to maintain

DOI: 10.4324/9781003230281-16

awareness, and avoid the moralistic top-down message that is often doomed to resemble the infamous garbled teacher voice in Charlie Brown's school.

Down With Luck; Up With Effort

Note

1. From *Habits of Mind Across the Curriculum*, Art Costa and Bena Kallick, eds, ASCD, 2009

16

Metastrategics

If metacognition is knowing how you know, "metastrategics" is knowing strategies for proceeding with a task. A student can learn how to use analogy to frame an argument or write a poem, but using analogy for solving problems or creating story plots requires a strategy. Knowing these strategies and others is a productive level of awareness that many students do not have.

The teacher can teach or help students discover strategies for solving social problems and mathematical problems, strategies for studying for a test, strategies for visually organizing before writing an answer to a test question, strategies for unlocking the types of thinking in a test question, strategies for writing free verse poetry, strategies for designing story plots, strategies for drawing, strategies for argumentation or debate, strategies for proofreading, strategies for cooperative studying, strategies for setting up scientific experiments, strategies for analyzing one's self, strategies for constructing theories, strategies for examining artifacts, strategies for appreciating art and music, strategies for improvisation, strategies for working in cooperative groups, strategies for improving handwriting, strategies for remembering, and strategies for applying productive habits of mind. Students and teachers could discover and practice these and many more.

DOI: 10.4324/9781003230281-17

Not knowing how to approach a task is a major barrier to success in school and life. A "metastrategic" learner knows strategies and the value of discovering and applying them.

Fish for a Lifetime

17

Not the Answer but the Plan

Imagine a science inquiry activity in which students do not seek answers but instead devise a plan of research. Questions could be posed such as the following:

How would you get wetter; walking or running through the rain?
How could you find out whether the cheetah is the fastest animal?
What is an effective way to learn a skill? A concept?
Which grass variety is the fastest growing?
How are conflicts best resolved?
Why do some people cheat?
Is altruism related causally to maturity?
What is the best way to memorize facts?
What motivates students in school?
What is a good way to relieve stress during test taking?
What can prevent bullying?

Students create or choose a question and individually and/or cooperatively design an experiment that can help answer it. The experimental designs are then written up and discussed with other students.

Practice Scientific Thinking

DOI: 10.4324/9781003230281-18

18

Teach Students How to Teach

To help create independent and persistent learners, teachers can teach students how to learn. In cooperative groups, students can also learn to teach each other. Learning to teach and be a learner at the same time can be a powerful advantage to students, both for their understanding of the content as well as for the skill itself. Using inductive teaching strategy and stimulating content (What causes earthquakes? Is this "weird fact" true? What is happening in this painting? What are some examples of conflict resolution in literature? Let's create a rule for determining the area of a triangle), students respond well to each other, particularly after think time and in pairs. Knowledge of the paths to learning and of strategies for teaching are two sides of the same coin—the currency for a lifetime of inquiry. Such knowledge frees students from overdependence and enriches the lives of everyone around them. As a consequence, the teacher is far less likely to function as high priest of knowledge and warden of behavior.

Every Class, a Methods Course in Teaching and Learning

DOI: 10.4324/9781003230281-19

19

Let Students Be Rule Makers

Too often, students are seen and see themselves only as consumers of rules and principles. The process of discovering for themselves these generalizations can make future application more likely. For instance, students learning the rules for quotation marks look for examples in written text, discover the pattern among similar examples, construct a rule, share it with a partner, help construct a class rule, return to textual examples to see whether the rule holds, and then apply it to their own writing. This example-to-idea-to-example-to-application learning process is classic and useful across content areas—for instance, in discovering mathematical formulas.

Induction Before Didaction

DOI: 10.4324/9781003230281-20

20

Student Test Making

Are we really clear on what students know after we test them? Certainly, we know what they don't know according to the test items we write. Or do we even know this? If the test items are worded awkwardly or in an inappropriately abstract fashion, we know only how well they can translate the prompts. Also, if the content is outside the students' interests or unexpectedly foreign to the teacher's purpose, they may be unwilling or unable to respond correctly.

Since the purpose of testing is to motivate students and to find out what they know, the teacher can have them write their own test questions of different types, or levels, at least for part of the test. Their questions can be in categories, and the teacher can approve them. Through this approach, the teacher encourages the students to become skilled or knowledgeable in certain aspects of the content. The students' mindset shifts from that of a guessing game to one of responsibility to learn something in-depth. Nothing is lost in content coverage since some questions will be of the teacher's choice. This "student as test maker" system is effective with classroom work as well. Students can write their own reading response questions, construct math practice problems, write questions for inquiry in science or social studies, and create their own assignments for written composition. The

DOI: 10.4324/9781003230281-21

passive stance that some students take toward their is destructive to their learning—skills, knowledge, and attitudes. Student-constructed tests and assignments will help turn the passivity into proactive ownership of the learning process.

Of the Student. By the Student. For the Student.

21

Note Making

Note taking is considered too much work by some students, a necessary evil by others. Elementary students rarely take notes in class or from readings; secondary students can find direct recall note taking to be tedious. Since to respond is to learn and taking notes is a form of response, how can note taking become more motivating and effective? One answer is to teach students how to take notes as true response rather than as rote recall or copying. True response entails placing information in a prior knowledge structure, or schema. This incorporating of knowledge is made possible by thinking about the information at various levels, or types, of thought.

When students are fluent with the seven basic mind actions of the **ThinkTrix** typology (see Glossary), for example, they can take notes as analogies, as causes or effects, as examples of a concept/generalization, as a concept/generalization from given examples, as an evaluation, as a difference/ distinction. (See examples in Appendix Figures A.11–13.) In other words, they can learn to operate on the information rather than simply feed it back. In classroom presentations, they can first write down information as given and then write their response directly afterward. For some, it may be possible to write the multilevel response during the presentation. If ideas don't come

DOI: 10.4324/9781003230281-22

immediately, they can write the questions they would like to answer. "What caused this? What will be the effects? What does this remind me of? What are some other examples of this idea? What is the concept here? Can one generalize from this information? Is the position ethical? Is there support for this idea? Is this fact or opinion?" Having a memory cue posted containing the types of thinking and/or questions will facilitate the multilevel response. One motivating variation is for them to color code the types of thinking at least in red and black, with red being multilevel personal response and black being pure recall. The teacher can allow the students to share their responses in pairs. Any group discussion or test that follows this process will demonstrate its educational value. Students will have learned to "reconnoiter" over text.

Treat Students as Thinkers

22

Hear It, See It, Say It, Beat It, Write It, Drop It

How about those spelling pre- and posttests? Do students show what they know on these? Are they a learning experience? A structured multimodality system can improve even pretest scores by 50%. The teacher says the word, places it in context, and repeats it. The teacher then hand signals the students to visualize the word (see it), repeat it subvocally (say it), beat out the syllables (beat it), write the word (write it). They then put down their pencils (drop it) until the signal for <u>write</u> on the next word. With this testing procedure, not only will students achieve better on the tests, but they will also learn more about how to spell on their own. After doing action research with highly positive results with fourth-grade students in an urban school, a Maryland University intern, Patricia Berard, labeled the approach the **VAT** strategy, for *visual, auditory, tactile* (see Glossary).

Test Student Knowledge, Not the Ineffectiveness of the Test

DOI: 10.4324/9781003230281-23

23

Spell With Two L's

"Al, my principal pal, went to the capital. Two c's and two r's occur in occurred. Ible, ible, ible irresistible. You will be embarrassed if you don't have two r's and two s's in embarrassed." Students enjoy learning tough spelling words through mnemonics like these, which will stand the test of time. The teacher can create a list of the 25 most misspelled words from student work or from a published list. After the teacher's modeling of the process of creating mnemonics, students can try to create them on their own. They then can keep their own inventions and/or choose those of other students. Here's one on the spot: "Lose the extra 'o' when spelling lose and set it loose." Students can probably improve on this one.

Loose, Don't Lose, Your Mind

DOI: 10.4324/9781003230281-24

Section II

Literacy—The Student as Reader, Writer, Speaker, and Listener

Literacy is a binding element of civilized behavior. The suggestions in this section are meant to facilitate the development of communication skills in every student. Reading, writing, speaking, and listening/processing are inextricably interdependent, and the school setting should be designed to make all four aspects of literacy increase the power of each. At the heart of the success of the school is the imperative that every student gain the recognized ability to succeed as a communicator.

The question to be answered is: *How can students best learn the crucial elements of communication?*

DOI: 10.4324/9781003230281-25

24

Unfluff Their Brains; Read to Them

In a *Winnie the Pooh* story Rabbit says, "Owl . . . you and I have brains. The others have fluff."[1] In reality, the way to the brain is Pooh. The Bear of Very Little Brain and his companions show us how to laugh at ourselves, ridding us of some of the prideful fluff that keeps us from thinking straight. Who among us can ever forget the books read to us by teachers, transporting us to other times and worlds? We forget some of the movies we see, but not the books read to us. In a sense we become the characters in the stories: Robin Hood, Amos Fortune, Charlotte and Wilbur, Johnny Tremaine, James and his giant peach, the children of Auschwitz and their paintings and poetry, "the boy" in *Sounder*, Harriet Tubman, the Athenians and the Spartans, Anne of Green Gables.

What ethical decision can we ever make without some influence upon us of the conglomerate hero of stories read to us? Knowing that there is something in the books for us is the surest motivator for us to read on our own. Unquestionably, teachers who read great stories to their students help create readers and a better world, less fluffy and hence less dangerous. "There was once a boy named Milo who didn't know what to

DOI: 10.4324/9781003230281-26

do with himself—not just sometimes, but always"[2] (*The Phantom Tollbooth*).

Let Them Find Themselves in Books

Notes

1. From *Winnie-the-Pooh*, A.A. Milne, E.P. Dutton, 1926
2. From *The Phantom Tollbooth*, Norton Juster, Epstein & Carroll, 1961

25

Reading as Seeing With Hearing

Recently, a first-grader marveled that she didn't know how she learned to read. She and many other young children have learned to read before they enter first grade. If they can learn to read without knowing how they did it, and even without their parents "teaching" them purposely, then perhaps the secret of *how* can be used in school. The secret seems to be that they have been read to consistently, are surrounded by books, and most importantly perhaps have had their eyes on the page as they listened to the reading. What better way to learn to read than seeing the words as one listens to them? Children, especially those without the home reading environment, benefit immensely when the classroom is outfitted with a listening center where they can hear and see the story as it is being read. If computers are available, programs are accessible that read the story aloud as children follow them on the screen. Every child, every day, can have this opportunity. If in addition the teacher surrounds the students with books, allows class time to read, assigns reading at home, and reads aloud to them every day, the classroom can also be a place where the children wonder how it is they learned to read. This is only fair to the students and even to the teacher, whose formal instruction will become miraculously more effective.

A Secret Hidden in the Obvious

DOI: 10.4324/9781003230281-27

26

Comprehension or Memory?

When students are said to be having difficulty with reading comprehension, they have usually been tested in part on what they remember. So aren't they being tested for recall? If so, then how does one recall what has been read? The answer would seem to be that one recalls what one has repeated or discussed. Certainly, this is true for most of us. This being true, students should discuss what they read right after they read if they are to be tested on what they remember and comprehend. This can be accomplished elegantly with partners retelling alternatively. Once the students have placed the reading in short-term memory, now they can be assessed for comprehension. The students can only comprehend what is remembered. After recalling, a sophisticated approach for deeper comprehension of important material would be to have the students metacognitively make up their own comprehension questions at levels such as the seven in the **ThinkTrix** typology (see Glossary). Then they can quiz/discuss/map them with their retell partners or answer them in writing themselves. Of course, the teacher can make up the questions or they may already be in the text or on the test.

Comprehend?

DOI: 10.4324/9781003230281-28

27

Novel Beginnings

How does an author begin a story? It can be argued that the first sentence of a story is the most important of all. As with great lines of poetry, students can look for great beginning sentences of books and develop a concept of what makes the sentences great. Also, they can try to write another first page from the selected first line and can create multiple first lines themselves from which to begin a story. A class collection of beginning lines can be posted from which students can write. With these activities, students are exploring the craft of a writer and coming closer to seeing how they could be writers themselves. The job of a teacher is then further realized, as the students see that writing is within their realm of possibilities. When the teacher or students publish excerpts of their quality work, the students learn to see their classmates in a new light—as cocreators, not merely as kids in school.

On Rocky islands gulls woke[1] Mr. and Mrs. Dursley of number four, Privit Drive were proud to say that they were perfectly normal[2] you don't know about me, without you have read a book by the name of The Adventures of Tom Sawyer, but that ain't no matter[3] once upon a time in Spain, there was a little bull and his name was Ferdinand[4]

DOI: 10.4324/9781003230281-29

as I walked through the wilderness of this world, I lighted on a certain place where there was a den, and I laid me down in that place to sleep: and as I slept I dreamed a dream[5] Where's Papa going with that ax?[6]

It Was a Dark and Stormy Night

Notes

1. From *Johnny Tremaine,* Esther Forbes, Houghton Mifflin, 1943
2. From *Harry Potter and the Philosopher's Stone*, J.K. Rowling, Bloomsbury, 1997
3. From *Huckleberry Finn*, Mark Twain, Chatto & Windus, 1884
4. From *Ferdinand, Monroe Leaf*, The Viking Press, 1936
5. From *The Pilgrim's Progress*, John Bunyan, 1678
6. From *Charlotte's Web*, E.B. White, Harper & Brothers, 1952

28

Verse Power

Poetry could be described as a palliative to the soul. If that is true, we ought to provide it for students. One intriguing way to soothe and feed the hungering spirits of students, as well as that of the teacher, is to find and bring to the classroom the currency of the great lines and verses of poetry. Once the students get the idea of a hunt for great verses or lines, they will bring them to class and share.

Break, break, break on thy cold grey stones, oh sea[1] two roads diverged in a yellow wood[2] a poem should be palpable and mute as a globed fruit . . . silent as the sleeve-worn stone of casement ledges where the moss has grown[3] here once the embattled farmers stood and fired the shot heard round the world[4] gather ye rosebuds while ye may[5] Quoth the Raven, Nevermore[6] in Xanadu did Kubla Khan a stately pleasure dome decree, where Alf the sacred river ran, down to a sunless sea[7] Tiger, Tiger, burning bright in the forest of the night[8] do not go gentle into that good night[9] and set you at your threshold down, townsman of a stiller town[10] the woods are lovely, dark, and deep, but I have promises to keep[11] I know what the caged bird feels, alas[12] but there is no joy in Mudville—mighty Casey has

DOI: 10.4324/9781003230281-30

struck out[13] steel'd was that soul and by no misery mov'd that from a father seiz'd his babe beloved[14] I'm nobody! Who are you? Are you nobody, too?[15] listen my children and you shall hear the midnight ride of Paul Revere[16] what happens to a dream deferred? Does it dry up like a raisin in the sun?[17] bury my heart at Wounded Knee.[18]

From the hunt for great lines of poetry may emerge a conscious love and a need for poetry.

Bring Down the Barriers

Notes

1. From *Break, Break, Break* by Alfred Lord Tennyson, 1842
2. From *The Road Not Taken* by Robert Frost, 1915
3. From *Ars Poetica* by Archibald MacLeish, 1926
4. From *Concord Hymn* by Ralph Waldo Emerson, 1838
5. From *To The Virgins to Make Much of Time* by John Waterhouse, 1648
6. From *The Raven* by Edgar Allen Poe, 1845
7. From *Do Not Go Gentle Into That Good Night* by Dylan Thomas, 1951
8. From *Kubla Khan* by Samuel Taylor Coleridge, 1816
9. From *The Tyger* by William Blake, 1794
10. From *To an Athlete Dying Young* by A.E. Houseman, 1896
11. From *Stopping by the Woods on a Snowy Evening* by Robert Frost, 1923
12. From *Sympathy* by Paul Dunbar, 1899
13. From *Casey at the Bat* by Ernest Thayer, 1888
14. From *To The Right Honorable William, Earl of Dartmouth* by Phillis Wheatley, 1773
15. From *I'm Nobody* by Emily Dickinson, 1891
16. From *The Midnight Ride of Paul Revere* by Henry Wadsworth Longfellow, 1861
17. From *Montage of a Dream Deferred* by Langston Hughes, 1951
18. From *American Names* by Stephen Vincent Benet, 1927

29

Poetry and Memory

Poetry is sound, rhythm, image, meaning. It is akin to music and can be both intensely personal and expressive. Its images can be guides throughout life, companions in joy and duress. Students can write it, read it, memorize it, recite it, and listen to it. They will adopt poetry as part of their lives if they want to, and therein lies the problem and the opportunity for teachers. If the teacher believes that every student can learn to appreciate poetry and even create it, then the problem of student motivation is on the way to the solution. Part of believing in the capacity of a student is for teachers to develop an appreciation themselves by reading and writing it themselves. For some teachers this is natural; for others, it is a stretch, but for the civilizing of students' minds, it is a necessity.

The classroom poetry should be relevant and understandable to the students. Dramatic oral reading as a daily occurrence is a way to begin. From the sound, images, and relevance students will soon sense the similarity between poetry and music and the connection to their lives. When they begin to bring in poems to share with partners and the group, the climate will shift. Lessons in prose writing can be interspersed and composed excerpts or whole poems can be published within the classroom. Another dimension, often lost like an Egyptian statue in the sand, is the

DOI: 10.4324/9781003230281-31

committing of poetry to memory. Students gain satisfaction from this exercise, despite some initial groans. The deeper they are into poetry, the more willing they will be to work at memorizing. When they move on to the next grade and more, the poems will stick with them, like songs. They will thank their teachers for this challenge and all the other work with poetry many years later. Poetry and the appreciation of it, thus internalized, will be an extra layer of identity and "voice" for the lucky erstwhile students.

I Had This Great Teacher Who . . .

30

Books—the Classroom Currency

The basis of all classroom success is the ability to read. This ability is gained by reading. Students have to have an appetite for reading. Much of this appetite depends on their choice of books. Along with reading to the class every day, the teacher can select books for individuals according to their interests. This process can be facilitated by having a database showing all the books that students can remember having read and the books they are currently reading. Both teacher and students can access this list to get ideas of what to read, connected to the names of classmates they can ask about them. After silent reading each day, students can take a couple of minutes to "sell" their books to partners. The teacher sets up the format for the selling so that not too much is revealed. Students can choose passages from their books to have the teacher read aloud dramatically to the class. This activity provides writing models for the class as well as interesting them in the books.

Since nothing gets done that doesn't get started, some classroom silent reading is essential if students are to be motivated to read at home. The classroom should house many books, and if the students have a school media center, it works well for the teacher to place popular/great literature out on a table. Students do not do well by searching through book spines. The keys to

DOI: 10.4324/9781003230281-32

creating the appetite for reading and a steady classroom current of books are to know what will interest each student and to know the best literature.

Reading—the Sine Qua Non

31

Book Reports

There can be no clever way to say "book reports." In the current idiom, they are what they are. Since there is no other way to name them and no hope of overthrowing them, perhaps it would help to adjust what is in them. The following are suggested activities that are truer responses to literature than those customarily found in, did I mention them, *book reports*. Students may

- ◆ Recreate scenes in writing by visualizing and feeling into the scenes;
- ◆ Construct a character web of a character with traits/ feelings and examples;
- ◆ Extract a moral or main theme of the story and explain why it is;
- ◆ From a list of other books/stories, find the similarities in theme;
- ◆ Decide what events shaped a character in the story;
- ◆ Describe some choices/choice made by a character and the effects of the choice(s);
- ◆ Choose a character from the story and compare him/ her to a character from another story, perhaps in a visual "ThinkLink";
- ◆ Create a plot design of the story, using from six to ten words;

DOI: 10.4324/9781003230281-33

- ◆ Create questions about the story for themselves or others to answer;
- ◆ Make questions from at least four thinking types;
- ◆ Answer in writing or visually one of the questions they ask;
- ◆ "Sell" their book to a partner without revealing the plot.

There are many other possibilities that students could choose, preferably in school, as they respond to literature. Notice, no mention was made of the "mood" of the story or the author's purpose. Apologies to the testing companies, we may have to choose at times between the lords of testing and true education. However, parents still may have to go to the store late at night for posterboards.

Responding, Not Reporting

32

Teach Through Stories

In one classroom in a school I've observed, students arrive every day expecting to hear the next episode of an ongoing fable told and acted out by their teachers. The two teachers spin a tall tale yarn every day, and the students live vicariously through the characters in the stories. They learn math, original writing, and history in relation to the stories. Teachers and students sometimes dress like the characters and engage other staff in the school in the adventures. Students generate episodes and have their own tales to tell. This is one example of a story-centered classroom—a plot that motivates and integrates.

What Comes Next?

DOI: 10.4324/9781003230281-34

33

Biblioallusions

In the allegorical film *Lili*, the puppet master's puppets each have a distinct personality. The dramatic struggles among the puppets are representations of the conflicts within the life of the puppet master, and by understanding this fact, Lili helps him become a more integrated person. Similarly, the teacher can use allegories to help students on their way to self-realization. There are two kinds of allegorical stories: ones in which the characters never change (*Lili*, *Winnie the Pooh*, Charlie Brown's *Peanuts*) and ones in which the characters develop (*Wizard of Oz*, *Charlotte's Web*, *Pinocchio*). Since we all share the characteristics of Pinocchio and his journey to realization and we all have a little bit of Piglet, Eeyore, and the others as part of our personality makeup, the students can see themselves in the characters.

The teacher and students can use literary allusion to help understand motivation and behavior in stories, in others, and in themselves. "Are you being the emperor?" "Is she being Cinderella to your wicked stepsister?" "Thanks for being Charlotte. We Wilburs appreciate it." "You are doing what Androcles did. I hope the Lion knows that." "Which Oz character do you feel the most like today?" "You are a regular Toad of Toad Hall. You have a new idea every day." These kinds of remarks constitute a kind of ethical, character-building, self-realizing shorthand.

DOI: 10.4324/9781003230281-35

Literary common reference points have a contemplative effect on students and teachers, as well as motivate all to read better literature. Fantasy literature is another source of "biblioallusion." This beats the moralizing and lecturing that can be part of every teacher's day.

Puppets of the Soul

34

The Reading Wheel

Years ago, researchers at Michigan State gathered together some master teachers and observed how they taught reading groups. They found that the teachers were not teaching students comprehension/reading response strategies, though the groups were well managed. One could speculate that the teachers didn't know the strategies. It is more likely that in the complex dynamics of the classroom, the teachers forgot to build in the strategies. Remembering in the classroom swirl is difficult for teachers and students.

The solution in this situation as well as in math and other content areas is to cue the strategies where everyone can see them. From this forgetting hypothesis emerged the **reading wheel** (Appendix Figure A.14) in Maryland, a teacher/student memory tool containing several key learning strategies. Not only does the wheel, with its three movable pointers, remind the teacher of what to emphasize in the lesson, but it also can cue the students on how to use their minds as they are waiting for others to finish reading or doing some task. On the inner orbit of such a wheel could be the following: *Role-play, Question, Pair Read, Retell, Predict, Visualize, Remember, Brush-Up Read, Respond by Analogy, Think Cause/Effect, Look Back, Think Link, Compose,* and several other possibilities. In the wheel's second orbit, or rung,

DOI: 10.4324/9781003230281-36

an explanation of each strategy can be written. It is also motiv-ating to establish hand signals for the response strategies. For the teacher to elicit a personal response to books in a dynamic group setting, remembering what to do is not always an option. Memory cueing is an effective ally for students and the teacher in an engaged classroom.

Forgetting—The Hidden Cause

35

Repeat for Fluency

Oral reading is motivating to hear and satisfying to do. However, "round-robin reading" violates the principle of maximum student engagement (Every-Student-Response (ESR)), as does students reading to the large group. A "repeated reading" strategy, known as "brush-up reading," between partners combines the satisfaction of reading aloud with an opportunity to improve fluency and to develop a sense of competence as a reader. The partners read a short passage silently, and then each reads the piece aloud three times to the other. After the second and third readings, the listening partner comments on the improvements in fluency the reader has made. This part can include help with a word or phrasing. The students then switch roles and repeat the procedure. In this way, the whole class is involved, and the teacher has an opportunity to assess and support by making rounds. Confidence and pleasure are both crucial in developing and accomplished readers. Repeated readings can help bring about confidence and pleasure, while at the same time allowing for the guided practice and self-evaluation that are necessary for success in any enterprise.

Students Helping Each Other

DOI: 10.4324/9781003230281-37

36

Character Relationship Analogies

Personal relationships contribute to many of life's joys and successes. It might be said that almost nothing is more important to students than their connections to others, particularly friendships. This fact, and the students' need to develop friendships, calls for an understanding of relationships through literature and drama.

One particularly effective approach to this acquiring of understanding is the use of character relationship analogies in which relationships are compared from one literary, film, or non-fiction context to another. To facilitate this strategy, students compile a list of relationships from books they have read or movies they have seen. Each student makes a private list, and the class agrees upon a class list from familiar stories. This list is placed on the wall. The students work individually and with partners to characterize the relationships. Charlotte helped Wilbur feel terrific, advised him when he made mistakes, consoled him when she had to go. This helper, or saving, relationship can be compared to similar ones in *Bridge to Terabithia*, *Pinocchio*, *Beauty and the Beast*, *Summer of My German Soldier*, *The Wizard of Oz*, *Helen Keller*, and countless other stories. The pair and group discussions that follow the recognizing of the similarities will reveal also the differences among the relationships (what kind

DOI: 10.4324/9781003230281-38

of "saving" in each of the stories?), as well as themes to look for in other stories. Students benefit by creating ThinkLinks, or visual organizers, to show the connections. A favorite visual is the ratio shape that shows a string of analogies in mathematical form (proportions) anchored together by a common theme. For instance, the emperor is to the scheming tailors as Pinocchio is to Fox and Cat as Wilbur is to some of the barn animals as Ichabod Crane is to Brom Bones, in that each is a "tricking" relationship. How and why each of these trickeries succeeded or failed makes for illuminating discussion. Students will have no trouble seeing the relevance to their own lives and to other stories.

No Student Is an Island

37

People Links

Multimodality experience cannot be easily forgotten. One strategy to test this proposition and to deepen student understanding of literature and life is to have them be living visual organizers—that is, link themselves together conceptually. For instance, if the theme, or concept, being explored is *freedom*, one student stands in the middle of a circle representing the concept and others space themselves on the circumference as examples of freedom in different books or movies. The students then tell what their respective freedoms are from—freedom from fear, freedom from hunger, freedom from captivity, freedom from bullying, freedom from tyranny, etc. Their testimonials can include the paths to their freedom, the effects of the freedom, their feelings during the struggle, their advice to others similarly constrained.

Other options are to act out a scene exemplifying the literary character's struggles for freedom. They could play all the parts, pantomime, or role-play with a partner. This kinesthetic "think linking" strategy has numerous variations, some of which students can invent. The teacher can participate as part of the design. Some possibilities are character studies with a single literary character in the middle and feelings or characteristics on the circle, cause and effect explorations using domino or tree root shapes, human Venn diagrams for similarities and differences, a

DOI: 10.4324/9781003230281-39

scale of justice for weighing right and wrong, or an event in the center and themes, causes, effects, or similar events on the perimeter. The teacher and students can follow up these dramatic exercises through discussion or written composition. The strategy works well for concept development in science, social studies, math, and any subject where understanding is the objective. Both memory and understanding are accomplished at once.

Being the Shape of Thought

38

The Story Theater Chain

A path to successful playwriting proceeds from the hearing, through telling, to acting out, to writing down. Thus, a chain of student involvement through several modalities provides the enabling structure necessary to make playwriting successful for students. Using a fairy tale, a fable such as Aesop's, a scene, or a familiar short story, the teacher reads or tells the piece aloud, dramatically. The students then tell the story to each other in pairs and act it out. The individual students then write the story down in dialogue. The writing down can be from a student's notes, or taped recording of the acting out link of the chain, or from memory. The students can then memorize lines from the plays and act them out according to the scripts. Polishing of the scripts follows. If all students are to experience success as playwrights, this "chain" is a necessary ingredient.

Let Students Be Playwrights

DOI: 10.4324/9781003230281-40

39

"Why Not Let Them All Act?"

The language arts visionary James Moffett once asked a very proud teacher, "Why not let them all act?" (Moffett, *Drama: What Is Happening*, NCTE, 1967). Two groups of four fourth graders had just acted out a scene from *Cinderella*, as the class sat as the audience. The famous observer thought they did well but wondered why the others had not had a chance. For the next scene from *Jack and the Beanstalk*, the entire class split up into groups of three and acted out the scene in spots around the room. Upon returning to the large group, most groups wanted to perform the scene for the class. From this day on, all improvisation of scenes from literature included every student. Later when the teacher worked with the class to construct with them a theory of improvisation, one usually reticent third-grade child said, "It was like swapping bodies."

"Why are my sisters so mean, Fairy Godmother?"

DOI: 10.4324/9781003230281-41

40

What to Write About: A Personal Question

Journaling is a term that connotes a journey. It is said that everyone's life is a novel, and that being so, every child's life must be at least a novelette. Successful writing in school from one's own experience requires at least two aspects: the ability to revisualize and to write from the memory, and the ability to remember the events in the first place. The former ability can be learned from seeing and practicing various models of scene writing, and the latter ability requires memory cues. For classroom or home journaling in which "trolling" for the past is required, students do best when they create a personal list of places, events, times, people, interests, and topics that can act as triggers for their writing. A great sapper of classroom energy for teachers, as well as students, is the inability to remember what to write about on the spot. These items can be on a personal list or a set of cards. They then are used as catalysts for writing that can match the student's mood of the moment and keep memory writing activities from falling victim to forgetting.

Write What You Know

DOI: 10.4324/9781003230281-42

41

History Writing

Fascination with history can depend on what history the students read and how it is written. Different depictions of the same event have different impacts on the reader. Differences can be in style, in emphasis on significance, in emotional impact, or in factual accuracy. An effective and enlightening exercise for students is to study a relatively minor event in history by reading accounts in several sources. They then analyze the accounts, choose the one they prefer, and explain to a classmate why they prefer it. Once this exercise has been repeated at least once, they write their own accounts of an event after reading several depictions and share their writing with other students cooperatively. The criterion for critique becomes the degree to which the writing interests others in learning more about the event. Style, significance, and emotional content are the key factors in arousing interest, and the "facts" are emphasized as subjects for corroboration through inquiry.

Beyond the value of students learning more about how to read history with a critical eye, putting them in the position of being historians contributes to their sense that they can be active contributors to knowledge. Additional exercises in writing out

DOI: 10.4324/9781003230281-43

events from their personal histories and analyzing them for style, significance, emotional content, and factual accuracy would further their sense that they can be historians.

Being in the Game

42

Use Parallel Plots

Children often write stories that are skeletal and episodic. One is reminded of the 100-word book report in the musical *You're a Good Man Charlie Brown*—lots of words on the way to lots of "the ends." To write stories, students need plots and plenty of them. It has been said that there are only four basic plots. Could these be exemplified by *Cinderella*, *Pinocchio*, *Beauty and the Beast*, and *The Emperor's New Clothes*? From these and other familiar stories, even nursery rhymes, students and teacher can create plot designs or maps. When these designs are displayed, students choose a plot, create a setting and characters, and begin writing. The result will be more satisfying than Charlie's 100 words and students' episodic stories. From *Romeo and Juliet*, *West Side Story* did spring.

To Avoid the Skeletal, Start with the Skeleton

DOI: 10.4324/9781003230281-44

43

"Transprose" to Poetry

A prose description written by a student can be reshaped into free verse poetry. After a student writes a description, the teacher can reshape the beginning of the prose into free verse, and the student is then encouraged to complete the pattern. The following is an example of this procedure, modeled by the teacher:

"The sun glistens on rocky cliffs which stretch seaward like gnarled fingers. Lumpy crags surround pools and are shadowed by evening clouds. They are countered above by white wisps of clouds, stretching away like the shore."

Sun glistens
On rocky cliffs
Stretching seaward
As gnarled fingers.
Lumpy crags
Surround caverned pools
Shadowed by evening clouds
Wispy
Countering above
Stretching, fading
Like the fingering shore.

DOI: 10.4324/9781003230281-45

The secret to teaching this process is pictures, pictures, pictures, prose description, and teacher modeling of the entire process. The hope is that teachers will "transprose" into free verse along with the student

Each Student, and Teacher, a Poet

44

Problem-Centered Story Design

One way to approach plot design in story writing is by providing/eliciting a list of relevant problems. The class assembles a list of problems faced by story characters and posts these. Starting with the idea that "your character has a problem," a list may include items such as the following:

He/she has a secret
She/he feels disliked
He/she wants to help a friend
They want to reach a goal
They have met an obstacle
She/he feels incapable
He/she has been tricked

When a companion list of settings is posted, students will have a motivating head start at story writing.

For Most Story Writing, Design Before You Write

DOI: 10.4324/9781003230281-46

45

Teach Craft Through Models in Expository Writing

Students do not generally do their best work on expository writing unless they have been immersed in models. Therefore, have students read (and read to them) multiple examples of essays, research reports, opinion pieces, analyses, or any other form that they are to attempt. When they are deeply familiar with the form, have them deconstruct the models and discover the organizing frameworks and the thinking paths. The overall question is, "What kinds of thinking are going on here, and how is the thinking organized?" Examples of specific questions might be as follows:

> Is the report hypothesis-driven or is it hypothesis-free? Is the essay thesis statement up front or is it to be discovered? In the comparative analysis, are the similarities stated first and then substantiated, or are the examples first described in order to reveal the similarities? Is the main rationale for the opinion one of cause and effect?

After this analysis of models, let them read and hear whole models again. Now they will be more able to write on their own,

DOI: 10.4324/9781003230281-47

having chosen topics relevant to them for audiences about whom they care. In the analysis of their work, avoid like the plague such worn-out, misleading, and tedious prompts as *supporting details, topic sentences, main idea, clincher sentences*, and *the five-paragraph essay*. Instead, focus on how the analogy holds up, how well the causes fit the effects, how coherent the organizing framework is, whether or not the examples fit the ideas. Any rubric should reflect the cognitive path of the writing. Also, for most expository writing, constructing a cognitive map, or Think Link, beforehand can lead to better results.

Teach Whole to Part to Whole to Application

46

The Verve of the Verb

A common perception among young writers is that the adjective, or "describing word," is the most important element in "colorful" writing. A strong case can be made that it is, in fact, the verb that is the strongest conveyor of the image. Though this contention is debatable, it is true that students tend to string adjectives out like beads on a string to the detriment of the flow of the writing. To give the verb at least equal billing, read aloud descriptive passages from literature that showcase the image value of the verb and make the passages available as models to the students. (The same approach can be used to demonstrate metaphorical style.) Then bring in several pictures depicting action, as well as still scenes from which action can be inferred. Model for students how to write several verbs that reflect some part of a picture and ask them to choose the ones they think best convey the image. On their own, they can do this exercise several times. Observation skills are the key here. (Note: A good source of models for scene writing is *The Describer's Dictionary: A Treasury of Terms and Literary Quotations, 2nd Edition*, by David Grambs and Ellen Levine, Norton Press, 2014.)

When students have had practice with verb choice, show them how to build a sentence around the best verb and set them on their own to create one-sentence descriptions. When they

DOI: 10.4324/9781003230281-48

have all done several of these, read their sentences aloud to them dramatically and publish or post some of the best work with their initials beside the sentences. If you have done a descriptive writing baseline assessment earlier, now give the same type of assignment again and see whether this training in the writer's craft has made a difference. It will have. "The musical flute sparkles the air around the Emperor of Rome" (J. B., Grade 4).

Teach the Craft Elements of Writing

47

Recreating Scenes

To learn to write, students must write. The question is, what kind of writing should they do in order to develop the underlying skill that will make all forms of writing more possible? Stories require plot design and are often written episodically. Essays are expository and are complicated exercises in thinking. What is the foundation of writing for communication and pleasure? If students don't see writing as a way to communicate and/or as a source of pleasure, they will not do it unless forced and then not well. It may be that one good way to learn the underlying craft of writing is to do scene writing, as in the following example by a fourth-grade child:

> Everyone was asleep. Everyone, that is, but the cat. The cat looked temptedly at the sleeping magpie. Then he started the journey up to the cage. Up the cupboard shelf. Soon the cat was at the top. He leaped forward into the air toward the dangling cage. He caught onto the cage. The magpie looked terrified. So did the wise old woman. The old woman tried to drag the cat off the magpie's cage. But no, the cat had tried days, for weeks and even months, and now he would not let go.

DOI: 10.4324/9781003230281-49

This recreated scene from *The Tower by the Sea* is one of hundreds written by elementary students from memory. Their assignment was to relive the scene in their minds and make it come to life either as a character within the scene or as an observer. They were not to describe it; rather they were to experience it and bring it to life in writing. This process is aided when the teacher reads scenes from literature aloud dramatically as models. Students are encouraged later to bring scenes from their own life to their writing. The results of personal experience writing and writing from pictures and memory will be obvious in the fluency with which they write stories and expositions.

Live It; Bring It to Life

48

See It, Be It, Feel It

Along with having strategies for bringing memories to the fore, students benefit from strategies of visualization, emotion, and point of view. The teacher models these orally and/or in writing by recreating scenes from life, film, or literature and then sharing how the mind works to recreate the scenes. Students are shown how to "see" the scene, moving like a camera lens to every object and at the same time using other senses. They learn how to be in the scene or observe it from the outside. As either a character in the scene or as an observer, they learn to feel the emotions, be they joy, puzzlement, conflict, sadness, or other. With this metastrategic coaching, they are learning the craft of a writer. The results will be highly motivating, adding a layer of identity to each student. All students are then more able to see themselves as writers, as people with something to say that other people will want to hear. When they do, school will be more of a real place where they want to be, rather than, as it sometimes seems to them, a place where they practice skills to please adults.

Here is a sample from a fifth-grade girl:

I better not let that Cinderella try on that slipper, it just might fit her. My daughters have to fit the slipper. They

DOI: 10.4324/9781003230281-50

just have to! If they don't, my life will be just ruined, just ruined. (Knock–knock) Oh, I better let him in.

Show Them How

49

Metaphor Training

Metaphorical, or analogical thinking, is the heart of creativity, poetry, invention, humor, plot design, problem-solving, persuasive dialogue, and other dimensions of what James Moffett called the "universe of discourse".[1] Given the centrality of this action of the mind, it makes sense to teach it as a skill, as well as to teach it in an integrated fashion as part of all inquiry, composition, and conversation. The "training" can be collecting stories of serendipitous inventions, reading and creating poetic metaphors, using analogies in debate and persuasive writing, analyzing and making puns and riddles, examining human imitations from the natural world, finding similarities in story plots, demonstrating the intersection of sets as a logical explanation of analogy, showing the power of similar problems in the solving of problems at hand, examining style similarities within and among the arts, developing cause and effect generalizations from parallel events, and other possibilities.

The metaphors and analogies that students find and create can be entered into a database and displayed in other ways so that they see themselves as knowledge makers and discoverers. Some of the figures of speech can become part of a greater whole as in a poem or a story; others can become part of a shared knowledge base for everyone in the class. In this daily activity lies the

DOI: 10.4324/9781003230281-51

potential for students building, and learning how to build, what Jerome Bruner called "structures of knowledge".[2] Here, as in other metacognitive activities, more independent, productive, and persistent minds will be the result.

Never Met a Phor That Wasn't Like

Notes

1. From *Teaching the Universe of Discourse,* James Moffett, Houghton Mifflin, 1983
2. From *The Process of Education,* Jerome Bruner, Harvard University Press, 1976

50

Essay Essence

Essays, ah essays. A concept bandied about, but who knows what they are or how to write them? Third graders are being asked to write them, as well as the high school students in "five paragraphs." Aside from the question of when such a form of writing should be introduced, there are the questions of what the various types are and how these should be presented to students. There is probably no one breakdown of the various types of essays, but teachers or a school system can settle on one to be used throughout the grades. Two such types might be:

- ◆ Essays beginning with a thesis statement/conclusion; an idea followed by anecdotes, cases, examples that support the idea. This is a common format for editorials. The path is from idea to confirming example. In science, "hypothesis bound."
- ◆ Essays beginning with a question and proceeding to try to answer the question through cases, anecdotes, stories. This path is from examples to concluding idea. In science, "hypothesis-free."

So then, there is either an idea confirmed and tied together by examples, or examples leading to and tied together by a common

DOI: 10.4324/9781003230281-52

idea. Is the essence of essay writing then tying together ideas and examples in a convincing or inquisitive written composition? If so, students should know this essence either by discovery from models or by being told and by their confirming this essence through examining models. The models can be made accessible or placed on the wall. Then, after each student makes a list of interesting topics, the writing can begin. Topics can require cause and effect thinking, making analogies, defending a point of view, exploring dilemmas, analyzing problems.

Let Students in on the Secrets

51

Essay Design

An inquisitive, hypothesis-free essay for elementary that can also work for older students can have the following parts: a question and listing of the stories to be examined in the first paragraph, and a second, third, and fourth paragraph in which the writer brings to life a scene from each of the selected stories. The scenes should in some way help to answer the question from the first paragraph. In a concluding fifth paragraph, the answer(s) to the question is stated and the three middle paragraphs are revisited for support of the answer(s). With the essay type in which the hypothesis is stated up front, the middle paragraphs are written to confirm the opening conclusion and the last paragraph makes the connection between the idea and the examples. Questions such as, "Why do people fake? What causes friendships? What are the effects of empathy? How are conflicts solved? What are the effects/causes of bullying?" are useful and interesting to students. This design will fit other content areas as well.

An extraordinary spin-off of the two types of cause-and-effect essays is a dramatization, or "essay theater," in which students act out the paragraphs. First, a narrator sets the question or the hypothesis, mentions the contexts for the next three paragraphs, and introduces the players by their role names in each of the following three paragraphs. The players then improvise scenes,

DOI: 10.4324/9781003230281-53

usually from familiar stories, that illustrate an answer to the essay question or that help support a hypothesis/thesis statement, depending on the type of essay. After the dramatizations, the students form a panel to discuss how the acted-out scenes illustrate the thesis or answer the question posed by the essay. The essay dramas can be rehearsed and performed for the class, or not.

The Emperor Was Fooled Because of Vanity

52

Model Quality by Excerpt Publishing

Nothing motivates student writers like seeing their writing in print. The problem for teachers in "publishing" student work is twofold—some writing is unworthy of the students, and even the best writing can be prohibitively lengthy. A solution for this problem is to select the best sentences, passages, or lines from the writing and make them available for all to read. Even poets and novelists can show you their best lines. When the teacher models the excerpting process, the students can learn to pick out their best lines or passages. If the teacher does a dramatic reading of the selections, students gain a deeper sense of the power of language and of their ability to produce it. To be writers, they have to know they can be.

Here are some student samples. A fifth-grade boy wrote,

The Knife! Twirling around and around in the water. Should he take a dive for it? Or should he stay in the raft and let his dog get torn to pieces by the shark? Wait—he had to save Uri who was his only real friend and companion. He had to dive down there and get his knife and kill that shark. Splash! Into the freezing cold waters.

DOI: 10.4324/9781003230281-54

And another from a fifth-grade girl:

Mafatu gasped at the sight of his knife diving deeper and deeper into the depths. Mafatu was thinking how long it took to make that sharp glittering prize and without it he would be handicapped. But suddenly it struck him. Maybe I could. The thought wilted in his mind. He could not make another knife. It would take too long. He would have to dive now! He hesitated, thinking of the depths he would have to dive, but he did!

Call Me Ishmael

53

Let Words Define Themselves

Words are best defined in the company of multiple examples. Asking for a definition prematurely can "sag" the discussion as the students fumble for the best way to frame the response, and that is when they actually have the concept. When they do not, the silence lasts even longer. Students learn better when they are asked with think time to provide examples of the word in context, sometimes after the teacher has given several examples. Defining is a complex process, and students can learn to define if the process is modeled.

Nevertheless, asking what something means and giving homework to define words and put them into one sentence is, and has been apparently forever, the favored approach to vocabulary development. Building conceptual understanding and a strategy for concept development are especially important for students who do not have regular access to higher conceptual conversation and reading. This teaching strategy, similar to concept attainment, can be framed as *example-example-example to idea to example*. Only one example and any premature rush to definition excludes many students and teaches none of them how to develop conceptually.

Teach the Discovery of Meaning

DOI: 10.4324/9781003230281-55

54

See the Sentence

Placing words in sentences is another time-worn-out activity. It makes sense to ask students to place a spelling/vocabulary word in context; what doesn't help their education is to allow them to write the sentences in a perfunctory, imageless manner. One way to make this activity a genuine learning experience is to teach them to make a picture in their mind as they write. Thus, the sentence "I have a <u>friend</u>" can become "I have a friend who helps me cut the grass." The sentence now has image value, and the meaning of *friend* comes more into focus. Likewise in this example, "He was a <u>cruel</u> person," the writer can visualize a cruel scene and write, "The girl was cruel when she showed her friend's diary to the other kids." As in all writing activities, the teacher models this visualization process over and over until the students' sentences come alive. By this process, students gain a sense of themselves as precise and competent writers, as well as learn the vocabulary.

Make a Picture; Then Write

DOI: 10.4324/9781003230281-56

55

Deconstruct and Reconstruct

Ah, "the main idea and supporting details." Students could generally care less about this important concept and hence the teaching of how to write a coherent paragraph can be frustrating. A solution? Have students diagram or map an existing paragraph by placing the idea or topic in a box and writing the supporting examples in dangling boxes below (refer back to Appendix Figure A.6). Then with the paragraph out of sight, ask them to rewrite the paragraph from the diagram. Some of their work may even be an improvement on the original. Practice this several times and then have them write their own paragraphs and practice the mapping process on these. The results in organized written thinking should be impressive.

Teach the Architecture of Thought

DOI: 10.4324/9781003230281-57

56

The Handwriting Game

Among the games students play, one annoying variety shows up in illegible handwriting. Admitting that penmanship is not too emphasized generally, at least the teacher and other students should be able to read the writing. Sometimes, students neglect to show how well they can write for fear that the teacher will expect their best handwriting all the time. If the teacher were to expect that, students might not be able to rush through the work. Still worse, they know that they might have to write papers over again. The counter game for this problem is to have students write a sentence in their absolute best hand, the same sentence in their next best, and a third time in their fastest semilegible writing. The teacher then places the samples in sleeves for the students to keep in their desks. The sentences are numbered 1, 2, 3, or "Handsome, OK, Timesaver" (see Appendix Figure A.15). In any writing activity, the students place the sample on the desk and wait for the teacher to say what number handwriting is expected for the activity. Game over, and school imitates life where adults write more or less neatly according to the situation.

"The Quick Brown Fox Jumps Over . . ."

DOI: 10.4324/9781003230281-58

57

Foreign Language Interest

Nothing succeeds like a memory of success, and students can learn to count from one to ten in several foreign languages. Their success in this counting will help them to see that they are capable of learning another language and that there can be a sense of accomplishment about knowing a different "code." This can easily be done through tape recording and repetition, as well as by having other student native speakers teach their classmates. Teachers can choose languages for which the school has native speakers, which will cast the native speakers in an expert light and ensure better pronunciation of the words. Students who are interested can go beyond the classroom five languages and challenge themselves to learn more through the internet or other students. All the learned language counts can be wall cued or placed accessibly. Also, students can learn greetings, questions, phrases, and other expressions common to all languages.

The teacher can encourage unusual languages, as well as the more widely-spoken ones. Songs can be motivating in the same way but are not always as possible to provide. The internet is one source of the languages. Further, the challenge of writing in languages symbolically different from English such as Chinese or Arabic can be motivating for some students. Students who have had this language learning experience will be more likely

DOI: 10.4324/9781003230281-59

to want to learn a language later, it seems reasonable to assume. What students do later on their own is some of the evidence a teacher needs that it has all been worthwhile.

Moja, Mbili, Tatu, Nne, Tano

Section III

The Voice of the Student— Honoring and Motivating the Individual

Students need to know they are there—that they have something to say, that someone cares, that they can be successful, that what they are learning has value, and that they can do things on their own. A classroom designed to give students the possibility to have this strong self-image as a learner and a worthwhile person is one in which true education will take place. The activities and ideas in this section are ingredients of such a classroom—one in which the "voice" of each student will be heard.

The question to be answered is: *How do students learn to respect themselves as learners?*

DOI: 10.4324/9781003230281-60

58

Relevance

"What is in this learning for me?" This is the unspoken question in many students' minds when a lesson or unit of study is presented. "What difference will this make in my life?" is another fair question implicit in student response to classroom activities. Sometimes the content and/or the presentation are so inherently interesting that students become motivated despite not sensing the relevance. At other times, the relevance takes time to be recognized, as in the cases of poetry or original writing. However, students' not having the need-to-know curriculum content can be a barrier to achievement at every level and in all subjects.

One path to the solution of this problem is for the teacher to begin every lesson by helping the group to think about the value to them of what they are about to learn. This can be done with a question or an explanation or both. Using Think-Pair-Share is a productive way to process the value of the activity. Thinking about value also can follow a motivating introduction or anticipatory set. A lesson beginning that engages the students cognitively, culturally, and even emotionally in more than one modality is often the key to their sensing the relevance of the material to their lives. The value assessment can also follow the

DOI: 10.4324/9781003230281-61

lesson. A focus on relevance and intrinsic motivation is crucial in all school settings, perhaps especially in less affluent or less academically inclined communities.

Make It Strange Cognitively and Familiar Culturally

59

Class Building Through Weird Facts

A classroom is a social system and as such requires a degree of social engineering. The best route for building a cohesive class is structured cooperative learning through which every student gets to know every other student. When this personal knowing succeeds, the animosities and cliquing diminish, and the academic and social goals can work together in synergy. Perhaps the best way to begin and maintain this bonding process is to consistently place the students together in pairs and change partners frequently.

To break the ice, an effective technique is to make the content of the pair interaction "weird." In educators' parlance, this means to have the students confront and discuss discrepant events and puzzling, unusual phenomena. When they discuss these conceptual incongruities, to them strange and problematic facts and ideas, they will forget the fact that they don't know or even particularly care for their partner. "Weird Facts" are a great leveler in the same way that humor breaks down barriers; in fact, laughter often accompanies the sharing of the unfamiliar content. To aid and maintain this process, students and teacher can establish a Curiosity Center complete with student-constructed lists, illustrated books, a computer, student projects, a video setup for

DOI: 10.4324/9781003230281-62

dramatizing the facts, and suggestions for how to inquire into the facts.

The facts that students choose to share with each other, and the thinking that ensues, open up the students to each other and to the teacher to an extent difficult to achieve in other ways. At least as important as the social benefit is the possibility that students will persist on their own to inquire further, perhaps even well beyond the school year. Intrinsic motivation is the fuel of learning.

Mind Building and the Sense of Wonder

60

Cooperative Learning

Teamwork has made America great. Depending upon and nurturing individuals free to develop ideas and skills, teamwork and its necessary cooperation are the foundation of progress. The marketplace of ideas and free enterprise is replete with calls for team players and critical thinkers. Despite the ideological back and forth, cooperation and competition are not dichotomous. Rather, each depends upon the other. All this is to say that the classroom should be a setting where cooperation is encouraged along with critical thinking and individual achievement. Effective cooperative learning is facilitated by the following:[1]

- ◆ Being preceded by independent thought, often in writing.
- ◆ Having engaging and relevant content as a focus of the cooperation.
- ◆ Having clear-cut and shifting roles for each student in a team.
- ◆ Having clear goals for teamwork.
- ◆ Having a rationale for the selection of the pairings and larger teams.
- ◆ Having several possible preset pairings into which students can easily shift.

DOI: 10.4324/9781003230281-63

♦ Making clear to students that they will be working in different teams.
♦ Having a repertoire of structures for cooperative interaction.
♦ Having a comprehensive organization.
♦ Having self-evaluative strategies for pairs and larger teams.
♦ Preparing for cooperation with team-building exercises.
♦ Sharing with students the rationale for teaming and the positive results.
♦ Identifying and practicing the social skills necessary for success.

Binding Together a Classroom

Note

1. This list is reflective of the comprehensive understanding of cooperative learning structures, technique, and rationale found in *Brain Friendly Teaching: Tools, Tips, and Structures* by Dr. Spencer Kagan, Kagan Publishing, 2014

61

Be Charlotte to Their Wilbur

Nine-year-old David (not his real name) was a danger to other students, bullying and striking out with and without provocation. Halfway through a frustrating year with David, the teacher learned that awkward, overweight David was an ice skater and drove his family's tractor. Inspired by necessity and E. B. White, the teacher took movies of David's achievements and showed them to his antagonistic classmates. David hit no one else that year. Like an image out of focus, children's better selves don't always show up at school. If they don't, the teacher may have to be the focuser.

You Are Who You (and They) Think You Are

DOI: 10.4324/9781003230281-64

62

Every Morning an Itinerary

There are some students to whom it is difficult for some teachers to relate. This cannot always be avoided. The reasons are varied. Sometimes these students want attention from the teacher or other students; sometimes they feel incompetent. They may want to establish themselves as powerful, or they may be experiencing difficulties at home or on the playgrounds. To solve the problem the teacher has to sort out the possible causes and build a response based on the best guess as to what the weighted causes are. Regardless of the causes, the teacher has to bond in some way with the student, which can be difficult, especially when the classroom is being disrupted.

One strategy that can work is for the teacher to plan a classroom "itinerary" each morning. The itinerary should target the most troubled students, as well as others in such a way that it is not too obvious. This can include discussing a student's interest, giving him/her a book that is designed to meet an interest, asking questions about outside activity, commenting with specific praise on something that happened the day before, sharing a "weird" or puzzling fact, following up on a previous conversation, and many other possibilities. The key is to reach the students before they begin a pattern of attention getting or disturbance. Students who receive this kind of before-class interaction are often less

DOI: 10.4324/9781003230281-65

likely to spend the rest of the day seeking the teacher's attention and may be affected in other positive ways as well. Planning the itinerary is crucial in that something often occurs that prevents spontaneous decision-making. Over time, the focus of some of the more difficult students will sharpen, the teacher's decisions will improve, and the classroom climate will be the beneficiary.

Find Them Before They Find You

63

Bring Forward the Big Ideas

With the students, create or find proverbs, sayings, principles, aphorisms, maxims, quotes, and hypotheses. Fill the walls with these statements and those of the students. The walls of the Jefferson and Lincoln Memorials have power because their inscribed sentiments are some of the buttresses of civilization. Put up the words that can hold a classroom, and someday maybe a world, together:

> Learn to read; read to learn. Might is not always right. Friendship is the glue. Cooperation is the ally of competition. Life is a journey, not a race. There is beauty in mathematics. Knowledge is power. There are some things in life you don't realize.

Sayings Are Life's Companions

DOI: 10.4324/9781003230281-66

64

Response-in-Kind

Praise, especially nonspecific praise, can leave students hungering for more, and when it is not forthcoming, they can feel let down. Precise praise may be effective, though the setting in which it can be delivered effectively varies from student to student. If inflated or given in a situation causing embarrassment, it can have unintended negative effects. Students want to be acknowledged, noticed for what they are doing, and they appreciate comments that show teacher interest or that lead to further improvement.

A highly effective teacher feedback strategy is for the teacher to "respond in-kind." This strategy is most effective when applied privately as in conversations or on written work. If the composition is about roller coasters, the teacher can write a note on fear of roller coasters; about animals, share a pet anecdote; about a friend, comment on how important friendship can be; about sports, write that the student's team has a challenge coming up; about a scientific experiment, write about a similar experiment. In short, the teacher shows interest in the content of the composition. Interspersed among the response-in-kind comments, the writer receives advice and specific praise. When they feel they have communicated with the teacher, students will be more likely to act upon the praise and the critique. In original writing, students want to know that the teacher is concentrating

DOI: 10.4324/9781003230281-67

on the message, not simply the flaws or even the expertise in mechanics. When the voice of the student is heard in this manner and in other ways, a "golden cord" connects the teacher and student. These cords hold everything together, give a boost, and will be remembered, sometimes for a lifetime.

Connect a Golden Cord

65

When Students Talk, Take Notes

Most students do not naturally view themselves as productive, creative, or original thinkers. As Art Linkletter put it about children, they do "say the darndest things." In fact, they say not only the darndest things, but they also say the profoundest things. If the teacher takes notes when students speak knowledgeably or sententiously and then reflects back to a student what was said, the classroom becomes a factory of knowledge, even wisdom. If some of their words are "published" or posted on the walls, a "poetic classroom" emerges in which the "voice of the student" is valued. The effect is that the students feel noticed and see their thoughts valued. Further, one enlightened and enlightening comment by a student can yield more data than a battery of tests. Watch them take class more seriously as they see you take what they say more seriously.

Honor the Voice of the Student

DOI: 10.4324/9781003230281-68

66

Conversations That Last

Students never forget private conversations with their teachers. Whether these conversations concern knowledge sharing, skill development, or even sharing of experiences, they almost always affect the student positively. In a large, dynamic classroom setting, students suspect that the teacher and other students do not know them well, do not respect their individuality. At all grade levels, perhaps particularly at the middle school level, students can feel like they are overlooked. Much of the counterproductive behavior in a classroom is caused by this sense of anonymity.

Some teachers overcome this tendency by holding regular discussions with individuals in which the students have an opportunity to participate equally. One example of this one-on-one discussion strategy is a teacher of a particularly complex middle school social studies class who promised students that he would hold three short conferences a day during independent work. The rules for the conversations included the opportunity for a student to bring up any subject within reason. The teacher could also broach a subject, but the student could change the topic at any time. A stipulation was that the students chosen for the conversations had to be managing their behavior. The teacher made an effort to overlook minor transgressions, knowing that

DOI: 10.4324/9781003230281-69

the students who needed the talks most were not always the best focused in the classroom. After a few months of these sessions, the classroom learning climate became markedly less "complex." Students no longer felt "invisible" to the teacher. Feeling known and noticed changed their attitude toward class work and, one might hope, toward learning.

Talk With the Leaders First

67

Affect, Its Effect

Students read faces. They sense atmosphere. What they "read" and sense tell them in some way how they are perceived, how they should act, whom they should trust. Nothing affects students more positively than a teacher's smile. As basic as this may sound, it is nonetheless true and not always easy to do. The press of classroom events is not always a smiling matter, but a positive countenance in the first moments of a day may lessen the press a bit. Time and time again, the author has witnessed teachers who despite some pedagogical weaknesses are working with cooperative and seemingly cheerful students. The attribute common to these teachers is a nearly omnipresent smile and clever personal asides to students. Of course, there are other elements involved, but the friendly and humorous disposition reflected through body language is clearly a factor. The adage, "Don't smile till Christmas" has a modicum of validity but may be partly responsible for no smiling till summer vacation.

Don't Frown till Christmas

DOI: 10.4324/9781003230281-70

68

Catch Correctness and Goodness

As teachers, our job is to correct errors and teach the students the correct way. This is all well and good but taken to an extreme is correction rich and motivation foolish. Supposedly efficient, this "correcting" gives little or no reinforcement for what students have done correctly. In fact, if students' work is too accurate, they may miss their chance to talk individually to the teacher that period. A productive approach is for the teacher to comment on what is right before correcting or having students correct mistakes. "You spelled four-fifths of this word correctly; circle what you think is your best-written letter or sentence; what part of the math problem did you do correctly?" If students feel that what they do right is noticed, they will be motivated to work harder to do their best work. The same is of course true for how they conduct themselves. It is all about being noticed, is it not?

Reward Part and Process as Well as Product

DOI: 10.4324/9781003230281-71

69

Test for What They Know, Not for How Well They Decipher the Question

Student achievement can only be assessed when students understand the questions being asked. Written questions that are age-inappropriately abstract or awkwardly phrased confuse students and therefore yield inaccurate data on what they understand or can do. When third graders are asked to identify the "major points of a passage," some may think the question is about soldiers or at best a boat trip. If these same students are asked to "tell the important ideas in a story," more will understand and reading comprehension can be more accurately assessed. Entire state testing programs have wrecked on these shoals.

If Assessing What They Know Is Important, Ask Them at Their Level, Coherently

DOI: 10.4324/9781003230281-72

70

Assessment Through Visuals

Both students and teachers profit by being aware of prior knowledge before the beginning of a unit of study. An efficient and motivating way to recall and show prior knowledge of a topic is to arrange that knowledge diagrammatically on a visual organizer. Web and concentric circle shapes are useful for this purpose. The teacher models this process several times by demonstrating how to go from topic to subcategories to other information. For instance, if the subject is colonial American history, subcategories would be wars, farming, family life, religions, entertainment, city life, Native American life, etc. Under each of the categories, the students write all they know in the boxes, bubbles, or circles. At the end of the unit of study, the students use the same visual organizer shape to write the knowledge they have gained. This visual pre- and posttest approach demonstrates to students and teacher what has been learned. Students can extend their writing in subcategories of their or the teacher's choosing.

What Did I Learn? Let's See

DOI: 10.4324/9781003230281-73

71

Make Math Talk Concrete

Students begin math in school with manipulatives and pictures. At some later stage, conversation and prompting in math switches to statements such as, "One-half divided by one-third and two times three." In making this transition from the visible to the abstract, it works well to pair/translate the more abstract wordings with more visual, or concrete, wordings, such as, "How many one-thirds are contained in one-half?" Or, "Two groups of three/three groups of two." It is worth inquiring into how much of math inadequacy is related to the "cognitive bends" incurred when the language of math isn't more gradually brought from the concrete depths to the abstract surface.

Take the Time to Say it Two Ways

DOI: 10.4324/9781003230281-74

72

Walk a Mile in Another's Shoes

For a society to function, its members have to support each other. Prejudice, greed, territoriality, "win at all costs" are all ingredients of societal dysfunction. Character education in schools comes down to one basic human quality: *empathy*. Education is universally recognized as the sine qua non of a civilized society and as such has to concern itself with the fourth "R": *relationships*.[1]

Given the universality of conflict, empathy is a necessary quality if people are to relate civilly to one another. Teachers know this or they wouldn't be teaching, but since the classroom is a microcosm of society, they really know it. Cooperative learning, bonding with students, motivation through relevant and interesting content, freedom for all to learn within structure—all are causative for good relationships. However, the importance of and disposition toward empathy can be learned explicitly within classroom activities. Toward this end, teachers use role-playing (method acting), examples from literature (*Anne Frank*; *Amos Fortune*), films (*The Red Balloon*), drama (*I Never Saw Another Butterfly*), theory building through multiple examples (What are the causes/effects of prejudice?), older students helping/teaching younger students, and opportunities for students working in the larger community as with underserved children. Transcendent purpose can guide children outside of

DOI: 10.4324/9781003230281-75

themselves to the service of others. If such service becomes a driving imperative in their lives outside of school, then society, the only one we have, will be enriched.

"It Is a Far, Far Better Thing That I Do . . ."

Note

1. Dr. Richard Solomon promoted the fourth "R" for relationships as a teacher educator in Maryland.

73

Mistake Collecting

A major obstacle to learning in school and elsewhere is the fear of making a mistake, coupled with the fear of other people noticing it. "You learn from your mistakes" is a meaningless phrase to the students at all performance levels who are saddled with this fear. Nonetheless, mistakes are helpful for learning if students have the habit of mind and attitude necessary to recognize and use them as such. For students to gain this knowledge, habit, and attitude, case studies of mistakes can be collected and analyzed. The teacher first models the value of mistakes as learning experiences by sharing several personal experiences. Some of these mistakes should be of an academic nature. When the teacher has thus demythologized mistakes as the enemy, students are encouraged to "collect" their academic mistakes by keeping a journal of them along with what they learned or could learn from them. Once these journals have been shared with partners and discussed, students can choose a mistake and the accompanying learning to write up to share with the class.

Knowing that classmates and the teacher make mistakes and have benefited from them may release the more fearful students from some of their concerns. When a publication of the mistakes is produced, the class is now ready to construct a "theory" of how mistakes can be useful. This theory can be made accessible visually on the wall. We should not underestimate the power of

DOI: 10.4324/9781003230281-76

negative dispositions to undermine the classroom as a learning community. Therefore, harnessing the power of the learning community to recognize the usefulness of mistakes is elegantly fitting. From this elucidating process, the class can spin off to mistakes made in literature and the wider world, and to ways to use/prevent/correct them through wise decision-making.

Read Books to Reduce Writing Mistakes, for Instance

74

Bridge In and Out

What did I learn? What was I reminded of? What is similar to this?

Every class can begin and end with these questions. Student response is crucial to memory and understanding. Not only will individual and cooperative responses improve recall of content, but they will encourage focus during the class activity. Students concentrate more on the knowledge for which they will be responsible, so give them three minutes in the beginning and the end of class to write down and share with a partner what they learned or considered important in the prior lesson/activity. To emphasize the importance and to reinforce their efforts, sometimes read the responses and comment on them verbally to individuals. This bridging, or debriefing, routine will replace the oft avoided "warm-up," or "drill," not to mention the negative symbolism of the gathering up of books two minutes before the class ends.

Say Goodbye to Pop Quizzes

DOI: 10.4324/9781003230281-77

75

Schoolwork at Home

Controversy surrounding "homework" ebbs and flows. Currently, the *flow* is on. Can something rational be said to give direction to schools? First of all, elementary and secondary school homework necessities differ. A high school student who wants to learn the content should work every weeknight to know and understand the next day what was presented the prior. This could take one to three hours. If more students did this and had to face a quiz in every subject for a few minutes the next day, achievement in the nation's schools would rise rapidly. Teachers could assign related tasks for home, such as research on the internet, but wouldn't have to every day. Studying for midterms and finals without responding daily to material practically guarantees mediocre grades and at least rapid forgetting. The same principle of nightly response to the day's work holds for middle school, with the inclusion of nightly reading and some original writing.

In elementary grades, studying material is less likely to occur and is perhaps less necessary. What *is* important is reading every night, drilling math facts, practicing cursive writing (yes, cursive writing in grades 3–6), some spelling practice, and an occasional exercise in original writing. Exploring the internet for interesting facts related to the subject areas can be assigned or encouraged.

DOI: 10.4324/9781003230281-78

Home assigned book reports and long-term research reports cause family dissension and can turn students off to school. There is a place for these within the class day, though literature response activities are more educational than the dreaded book report.

Two procedures are helpful to achieving compliance with homework. These are letting elementary and middle school students begin the homework briefly in class, the principle being that what doesn't get started doesn't get done, and placing the students in partners the next day to share and compare their homework while the teacher listens in, bringing social reward, teacher attention, and classmate support into the mix. These are of course just some thoughts, the points being not to let excessive homework turn young children's home life into a second formal school and not to allow the older students to be unresponsive to what they are learning.

Home as an Ally to School

76

Know Thyself

Socrates had it right, but did he know *himself*? This question is asked in the realization of how hard it is to know ourselves. We may even be our own hardest person to know because of the defenses built up that fend off the truth. This being said, teachers' first commandment is to face who they are and adjust attitudes and behavior to fit the complex mix of circumstances in the classroom. How to do this? A personality test such as the Myers-Briggs is a place to start. The match and mismatch of personality preferences can be funny and useful only when they are understood, and the classroom is rife with dynamics relating to the differences in personalities.

Once understood, the teacher can use knowledge of the similarities and differences to do some valuable social engineering within the class. This engineering should include how the teacher should relate to certain children differently. The Rokeach Ambiguity Scale (tolerance for ambiguity) was designed to help explain why some Radcliff students couldn't stand certain professors whom other students liked. When John Holt (*Why Children Fail*) began one class at Harvard, some students rebelled immediately because of the loose structure. Perhaps John knew more about education than he did about himself and about why that knowledge matters to a teacher. More important for teachers

DOI: 10.4324/9781003230281-79

than knowing their personality preferences, since that know-ledge can become academic, is that they ask themselves every day: "How does who I am and what I do relate to the successes or failures of the day?" Having answered this question, they can build the answer into the next day's plan. What the students are doing and learning is the issue, and if the teacher's personality and skill level are getting in the way, then she/he should adapt. Without a teachers' self-knowledge, the causes of problems will usually seem to lie outside the teacher.

ENFP

77

Avoiding the Deadly Intersection

There are problems in teaching that can be solved when the causes and their interactions are recognized. A common sign of one such problem is the dominance of discussion or cooperative groups by a few individuals and the reticence of the rest. The "kingdom" appears, once again, to be asleep. Since there is value to cooperative learning and group discussion, however, it is crucial to note that there are at least four factors contributing to the lack of focus in the activity and that these factors form a deadly intersection or counterproductive confluence. These are, at least, lack of interest or sense of relevance, lack of time to think, lack of clarity, and a low sense of urgency.

Replacing these factors with positive influences will make the intersection a more productive learning space for all the students. If the topic, or prompt, is in some way problematic, puzzling, or relevant, interest will be aroused. If there is structured time to think or write individually, answers will be rehearsed and hence more accurate and elaborate. If the language of the topic or question is clear, the students will understand how their minds are to work to respond. If the students know they may be asked to respond later in writing to what is being said in the discussion, they will feel more urgency to participate. These four positive actions, built into the activity every time, along with occasional

DOI: 10.4324/9781003230281-80

pair learning, will rechoreograph the classroom toward the inclusion and improved achievement of all the students.

Interest—Think Time—Clarity—Urgency

78

Beware of Myths

There are stories told to us and that we retell to ourselves. Some of these are untrue or only conditionally true. These stories have lasting power, standing the test of time, often unexamined. Examples in education are as follows: Students need to practice listening skills. (Have you heard of any?) Everything goes back to classroom management. (What does classroom management go back to?) We have to prepare students for middle school by teaching parts of speech (Is that possible?) Don't smile till Christmas. (Have you tried this?) What was the author's purpose? (Would E.B. White have answered this question?) What is the mood of the story? (Why ask this?) What are the supporting details? (The color of a shirt?) The solution? Treat old saw maxims as hypotheses, not as gospel. Create your own principles by analyzing your own classroom events.

A Teacher Is Not a Friend?

DOI: 10.4324/9781003230281-81

Section IV

Banks of the River—Classroom Flow for the Engagement of All Students

For a learning community to function productively, structure is essential. The classroom day can be visualized as a series of time segments of varied durations. Learning occurs within the segments, and the borders of the segments must be clearly defined. When such a system is in place, academic learning will likely be enhanced. With these borders and a transactional strategy for making them clear to students, classroom dynamics become manageable. The suggestions in this section are aspects of a structured system that allows for creativity and academic achievement.

The question to be answered is: *How can a learning space be designed to bring freedom to learn and structure into an effective balance?*

DOI: 10.4324/9781003230281-82

79

A River Needs Banks to Flow

The best teachers know that the structure vs. freedom, teacher-centered vs. student-centered, frontal teaching vs. cooperative learning disputes represent false dichotomies. There can be no true educational freedom without structure, and structure without freedom is custodial. Therefore limits, signaling systems, prescribed formats should coexist with visual, auditory, kinesthetic, tactile, curiosity-inducing, and relevant activities. Lessons "flow" in segments that require transition borders and mutually understood transition cues, as well as worthwhile content.

Avoid Floods as Well as Dried Riverbeds

DOI: 10.4324/9781003230281-83

80

Every-Student-Response

The ultimate goal of every classroom moment is to have what some call "Every-Student-Response" (ESR) and others "the engaged classroom." In order for the teacher or others to gauge this condition, it is useful to answer three questions. These are as follows:

To what extent is each student engaged/focused?
What percentage of the class is engaged at a given moment?
How worthwhile is the activity at hand?

The first question can only be properly addressed when all the modalities of learning are considered. These are **visual**, **auditory**, **kinesthetic**, and **tactile**. When a fifth factor is added, **relevance**, the best acronym is The **VAKTR** factor (also mentioned in Section I, Idea 22, "Hear It"). This question asks how much of the whole person is involved.

The answer to the second question shifts, as in the case of the first, from moment to moment. The issue here concerns the trend line and the individuals in the group. Is the tendency toward a stable or higher percentage of the class being engaged, and, secondly, which students are not engaged and why. The teacher can only play for high percentages and analyze. The quest for

DOI: 10.4324/9781003230281-84

perfection exhibited by some observers is unrealistic and demoralizing. "There was a child over in the corner who . . . "

The worthwhileness of the activity has three dimensions: the relevance of the activity as perceived by the student, the intrinsic motivational power of the activity, and the importance of the activity to the student's education. In other words, is the activity motivating, of educational value, and is it seen as such by the student? The criterion of Every-Student-Response is more positive and productive to apply than "classroom management," a term which is best perceived as an outcome of skillful attention to the three above dimensions.

Most of Each Student, Most of the Time

81

Planning by Template

Lesson planning is an essential element of teaching. The question is: What are the important elements of planning? Of course, the objective, the activity, the method of assessment, etc. are boilerplate. Aside from providing a framework, however, these elements do little to guide the planner's mind as to how the students are to think as they learn or what activities/instructional strategies will facilitate the learning. As in many classroom situations, memory doesn't always serve the teacher or the students.

The problem of thinking of what to do and how to do it can be solved in part by using theory-practice templates. With these predesigned templates, the teacher can remember the general categories into which the lesson will fit. For instance, a concept and skill development model (see Appendix Figures A.16 and A.16a) reminds the teacher that the strategy for teaching a concept can proceed from the specific to the general or from the general to the specific or both. Reminded of how students might think in the activity, the teacher selects one or both strategies. With the teaching of a skill, the template reminds us that the skill can be taught part to whole or can start with the whole and proceed to the parts. In planning, therefore, it is the mind actions and **content directions** (see Glossary) that students will take for which the teacher plans. For instructional dimensions,

DOI: 10.4324/9781003230281-85

a concentric wheel can include the key teacher considerations. For instance, bonding, connecting knowledge, student cooperation, motivating, teaching how to learn, assessing, evaluating the objective, allowing time for thinking, managing transitions, giving breaks, and being flexible are crucial elements of effective teaching. These can be on a template like the "B Wheel" (see Figures A.17 and A.18), a teacher tool that is useful for evaluating teaching, as well as planning a lesson.

Memory Tools as Planning and Evaluating Guides

82

Allow Think Time After a Question; This Isn't "Jeopardy"

In many classrooms, much of the time, hands go up after a question and the teacher calls on a student as quickly as possible. The educational and behavioral effects of this standard recitation model practice are negative indeed. By structuring a three-second, hands-down interval for thinking, the teacher can expect more hands to be raised, higher-level and more accurate answers, more students listening to each other, and more focused behavior. This three-second or more rehearsal time for students gives the teacher time to improve the clarity of the question, plan next steps, think about the answers given before, and scan the classroom. Thoroughly supported in research and known as Wait Time 1, this thinking interval is the cornerstone of an inclusive and engaged classroom.

For the Want of Think Time, a Classroom Was Lost

DOI: 10.4324/9781003230281-86

83

All the Wait Times

Given the prevalence of discussion in classrooms, a thinking segment after a question may be the most influential instructional variable in a school day. The effects are numerous, heavily researched, and easily recognized. Teachers have learned what the original Wait Time researchers may not have, that think time requires hands down and a think-end signal for hands to be raised. With this technique and the students' expectation that they may have to write the thinking and/or talk to a partner, a thinking opportunity is in place for all students.

There are two other less recognized and more difficult to implement Wait Times—**Wait Time 2** and **Wait Time 1 and 1/2** (see Glossary). Wait Time 2 is the interval between the student's response in the share mode and the response of the next speaker. The research on this variable shows it to be even more important than Wait Time 1. The difficulty in implementing Wait Time 2 is threefold: managing the end of the student's response, the signaling for the next response, and focusing the thinking. The teacher can manage the end of a student response by signaling or a verbal acknowledgment. When other students know that they cannot raise their hands until the teacher gives a signal for another response, they will not wave their hands or blurt out. To direct the students to think about what the prior student has

DOI: 10.4324/9781003230281-87

said, the teacher can divide the Wait Time 2 into two parts: one to think about what they just heard and two to think about what they want to say.

Another script the teacher can use after a question or a student response is to hand signal the type of thinking the students should do, such as cause/effect or analogy. Wait Time 1 and 1/2 is the time after students have done pair talk so that Think-Pair-Share becomes Think-Pair-Think-Share. The multiple think time, multidimensional orchestration of discussion has three requirements: students must understand the reason they are doing it; the teacher must believe with conviction that the strategy is essential to engaging all students in learning; the routines must be practiced and consistent. The positive results will have a multiplier effect throughout the classroom day.

Enlarge the Thinking Space

84

Setting of the Cornerstone

Classroom discussions are often not productive discussions but rather exercises in public speaking, opportunities for the most verbally skilled or extraverted to speak, or Jeopardy games where the fastest hand is called on. The best approach to defeating this pattern is the consistent use of Wait Time. Besides the teacher having to perfect the technique and being determined, the students have to see the value of the paradigm shift. Earlier grades will generally buy-in quickly, but older students have an unconscious interest in keeping the classroom interaction the way it was.

To bring the grades 3–12 students on board to support Wait Time, the teacher can elicit from the class what annoys them about the recitation model. When they have shared their concerns, such as "the teacher always calls on the same kids; quieter kids don't get a chance; I don't have a chance to think; some kids go on and on; I can't speak when I disagree; I can't hear the speaker," the teacher then suggests there is a solution to all the annoyances and that it is structured *think time*. After demonstrating structured think time several times, the teacher again elicits what the students noticed as effects. The effects are listed, and the challenge is issued to add new effects after the class has practiced. The teacher can set up action research models

DOI: 10.4324/9781003230281-88

with pairs of students as observers. One inquiry could count how many students are looking at the speaker during sharing. Another dependent variable could be the number of hands going up after a three-second think time as opposed to how many are raised with one-second unstructured think time, controlling for the difficulty of the question. A third inquiry could be how to the point or accurate the answers are between the two groups. A fourth study could investigate the types of questions being asked. Results of the studies, along with the friendly competition between teacher and students as to who conforms best to the cueing system, can convince students that Wait Time 1 is in their interest. Now pair talk and Wait Time 2 can be introduced with more student-led research.

Get Them on the Side of Maximum Participation

85

Whole Before Part

Important skills need to be seen in context before students are instructed in their use. One would do better in learning piano notes and chords by first hearing music or learning soccer skills after first seeing a game. Writing essays or research reports without first reading model examples leaves a student unnecessarily perplexed and unmotivated. A testing-driven tendency to focus on parts ("rush to rubric") before students have examined several whole models leaves students unable to produce quality products and unable to use or disinterested in using the rubric, or parts, to plan or evaluate their work. The importance of using whole models applies to all forms of writing, as well as to problem-solving and other forms of inquiry.

Don't Teach Swimming on a Dry Dune Far From Water

DOI: 10.4324/9781003230281-89

86

Think-Pair-Share . . .

Maybe the paradigm shifted when three extraverted students controlled the class discussion, or when students could recall very little about an inspired teacher presentation, or when students seemed to care less about what a fellow student was saying, or when the unfocused fringes of the class became unruly. The shift was an elegantly simple cooperative learning technique dubbed **Think-Pair-Share**. Now used fairly universally, the technique is one in which the students listen, then think independently for at least three seconds, then sometimes respond with a partner, and then sometimes share their answer or that of their partner with a larger group. The teacher or students can be in charge of the interaction, grades K–13. Despite the simplicity, teachers have developed details and variations. Some of these are as follows:

- ◆ The think time (Wait Time 1) is up to 10 seconds, rarely more, usually less.
- ◆ In writing, think time is longer. Students should always be ready to write.
- ◆ After the think prompt, hands are down until a cue is given to pair or share. Cues can be hand signals, a bell, or a visual cue.
- ◆ If hands go up too soon, the leader uses a hand erase signal.

DOI: 10.4324/9781003230281-90

◆ Pairings can be premade and varied. Pairs can turn into squares.

◆ Between pair talk and the share mode, transition seconds are necessary.

◆ After the pair mode, a few seconds can be cued for gathering thoughts.

◆ Think time is always; pair and share are up to the leader or teacher to call.

◆ Pair talk can be structured in many ways. These possibilities are wall cued.

◆ The teacher can move around to listen to the pair talk.

◆ The share mode can be shorter or omitted since response is the goal.

Teach Multimode

87

Put it Into Hands

Signal, for flow. Students are being asked to move as a group from one question, one response, one activity, one segment to another. These transitions can be accomplished by an agreed-upon set of transactional cues. In the elementary grades, especially but not exclusively, students and teachers can cue the shifts with hand signals. Also, hand signals can indicate modes of response, types of questions, degree of understanding. Imagine an engaged classroom in which students signal the types of thinking they or others are using, their agreement or disagreement, their understanding or lack thereof, their readiness to move on, the strategy they are using within cooperative learning groups. Imagine also the teacher signaling for the requested response mode as with Think-Pair-Share and with a multimodality spelling test. Transactional and **substantive sign language** (see Glossary and Appendix Figure A.19) as a signaling system is a key element in an engaged, Every-Student-Response classroom.

Everyone on the Same Page

DOI: 10.4324/9781003230281-91

88

Be Neither Concrete nor Abstract
Be Connected

Clarity is a result of coherence, and coherence is connected-ness. In all concept learning and communication, ideas must be connected to examples, concrete to abstract, general to specific, principle to case. Otherwise, teachers as well as students are set "cognitively adrift," unable to connect experience with conceptual frameworks. When abstract ideas and concrete examples intersect, a concept can be learned, or communication can take place. Whereas students should learn to do the connecting, teachers must do the modeling as they ask questions and teach concepts. Examples must "stand under" ideas for **understanding** to occur. At stake is conceptual, and hence intellectual, upward mobility for students.

An Example Without an Idea Is Like a Ship Without a Sail

DOI: 10.4324/9781003230281-92

89

Translate

What is not connected will not be clear. What is not clear will not be understood. When asking questions, word them two ways so that everyone can understand. When asked to measure the surface of their desks, only three fourth graders knew what to do. When the teacher translated *surface* to *top* of the desk, all the students began measuring. Every oral direction or thinking prompt can be worded two ways. The confusion, or "cognitive drift," is reduced when the higher abstraction, or concept, is comprehended and learned by its association with the familiar term or thinking type. For example, when asking students to summarize, translate by specifying that you mean either the most important ideas or the key events. When asking for a hypothesis, pair the question with the terms *cause* or *effect*. Do this consistently and watch the focus and the answers improve.

Don't Be the Garble Talk Teacher in Peanuts

DOI: 10.4324/9781003230281-93

90

Wake the Kingdom
Make Expectations Clear

One of the reasons a class or a group responds in a discussion as if it were a kingdom asleep or an unprincely frog on a log is that the students are not sure what the teacher's question is signifying. Is there one answer to the question? Several? Should they know the answer? Does the teacher know the answer? The teacher can clear up the mystery by signaling to the students the answers to these hidden conundrums before they respond. This tactic together with think time, teacher and student metacognition, student questions, intriguing and worthwhile questions, response writing, and pair talk will wake up the kingdom and crown the frog for sure. The hero here is not magic but rather the science and psychology of teaching in group settings.

The Prince Is Science; the Frog Teaches as He Was Taught

DOI: 10.4324/9781003230281-94

91

Student Learning Seconds Lost

In a discussion group of ten students, the teacher asks a question, and no hands go up. In ten seconds, a student answers, and the teacher asks for him/her to elaborate. There is a five-second silence and another student gives an off-base answer. The teacher rephrases the question. No hands are raised. Since the initial question, 40 seconds have passed. This elapsed time multiplied by the ten students equals 400 seconds, or 400 student learning seconds lost (**SLSL**). Given the prevalence of this type of lesson sag, the amount of unfocused lost time could equal the amount of time that would be available in an extended school year. Imagine the time lost when lost seconds are multiplied nationwide. Though counterintuitive to some, three seconds of hands-down Wait Time after the question and an accessibly phrased question would rechoreograph this scenario. The structured time would then serve the learning. To answer and to care about the answer, students need unpressured time to process the question, an understandable question, and sometimes even a chance to rehearse it with a partner before most are willing or able to speak.

Time, You Thief

DOI: 10.4324/9781003230281-95

92

Metering

Activities are going on in the classroom and the teacher is meeting with a small group. Assuming even that the class activities have been started and the students were focused from the beginning, how is the teacher to encourage the class to maintain focus while at the same time engaging the small group? There is no one answer to this classic situation, but there is one that has been proven to work well. The technique might be called *metering*. Assuming that students work better when there are eyes on them, the teacher or students can design a focus meter that the teacher can manipulate throughout the upfront discussion. A glance at this meter, perhaps in the form of a giant thermometer (taskometer?) or a wheel in segments, tells all students in the room what percentage of them are on task. The teacher adjusts the meter with periodic looks around the room.

Since the key to concentration in a classroom is students getting started, and anathema to focus is disruption, the times after the students try to raise the meter upward take on an on-task life of their own. The "concentration bubbles" pop far less. Metering has other uses such as with room cleanup when students work against the clock to clean the room and establish record times. The teacher brings hands together as the meter. As

DOI: 10.4324/9781003230281-96

with all transition and activity signaling, the secret for the teacher is conserving personal energy, an easily spent resource. Energy is conserved by keeping persuasion out of the transitions.

Work to a Standard, not for a Command

93

Ride the Wave

Classroom activity is dynamic. One characteristic of this dynamism is that the action sometimes moves in waves. The teacher often has to use the rhythm of the wave or risk being thrown on the metaphorical beach. Examples of "riding the wave" effectively are allowing students to briefly socialize and put down their books before beginning a class session, allowing the buzzing to continue and die down after an interesting teacher question, starting a line of students moving when most of the students are ready instead of waiting for perfection, being sure that all students have started working before the teacher's distracted by an individual student, allowing natural laughter to die down rather than trying to cut it off immediately, not insisting on total quiet when turning to write on the board, using turning around to face them as the cue for quiet. In general, the principle is not to hold on to impossible dreams that run counter to the natural flow of the classroom. Instead, use the flow of energy to move from one segment to another, cueing transitions when the "wave" has hit the beach. If a tsunami keeps returning, look to other causes.

Use the Natural Dynamic

DOI: 10.4324/9781003230281-97

94

Keep the Horse in the Barn

Research has shown that once disorder has claimed a lesson or a classroom, all teachers have difficulty restoring it. The distinguishing feature of effective teachers is that they can prevent disorder. The term *classroom management* is an overused term and at least should be considered more of an effect than a cause. ("He is having difficulty with classroom management.") Disruption is caused by much more than a lack of organization, structure, and firmness, the most commonly attributed factors. Adherence to instructional principles and a caring climate are at least equally important. The teacher who sees the goal as maximum response from every student and who sees instruction, management, and positive climate as equal partners toward that end will keep the horses in the barn, or depending on the difficulty level, at least in the field.

Prevention Is the Key to Order

DOI: 10.4324/9781003230281-98

95

Old-Fashioned Seating, With a Twist

Oh, those rows of nailed-down desks, facing forward. Weren't they awful? And the nice tables with dinner table seating; aren't they liberating? The answer to both these questions is *yes*, but with qualifications. The single widely spaced seats facing forward are ideal for independent work and for focus on the teacher. The tables facilitate cooperative work and projects. Since there are times when cooperative work is required, other times when silent independent concentration is necessary, and times when class discussion with teacher focus and student-to-student discussion are called for, how should a teacher arrange seating? There is no one answer to this question, but two arrangements have been shown to work. These are pairs of desks facing forward and a concentric horseshoe-shaped design.

The pairs facing forward allows for independent work with a minimum of peer interruption, as well as cooperative learning in pairs. The desks/chairs can be swung around to create foursomes. The focus on the teacher is easier, but eye contact with peers in large group discussions is more difficult. The concentric horseshoe pattern allows for pair interaction, focus on the teacher, and eye contact in class discussion. Turning desks/chairs into groups of four is also an option. Though the arrangement is dependent upon subject matter (for instance, art, science, and K–2 may be a

DOI: 10.4324/9781003230281-99

better fit with tables or desks facing each other), flexibility is preferred over locked-in (or nailed-down) extremes. Independent
classroom work and teacher-focused instruction or directions do
not fare well when students have eye contact with each other
at tables. This fact is easily observable, and the argument that
cooperative learning is hampered with other arrangements is
hollow. Without independent thinking and the ability to focus
on the teacher, cooperative learning cannot succeed.

Concentration With Cooperation

96

The Nine A.M. Letter

A teacher once received a letter at 9:00 A.M. from a parent who asked the question, "Are you running a correspondence course with my son?" After fuming around, the teacher was advised by a wiser colleague to settle down and consider what the parent was saying. Further advice was to determine to what extent the parent had a legitimate criticism, call the parent in for a conference, and begin by agreeing that the able student had been left to proceed with the math on his own with minimum teacher input. This was done and a plan was made for the teacher to check in with the student on a more regular basis. The parent was then asked to write or call, but not at 9:00 A.M. since the timing was unnerving. The parent agreed and the matter was concluded. Several months later at a PTA meeting, the father stood and praised the teacher on several aspects of his teaching. The moral to this parable is that first find where the criticism is valid and then voice any concerns about its content or the method of delivery. This principle gained from this experience was a key factor in the teacher's future relationships with parents.

First, Determine Where They Are Right

DOI: 10.4324/9781003230281-100

97

Notice Students at Beginnings, Endings, and Outside

A teacher once said, "They don't know they are there until I notice them." This insight holds true since students tend to see themselves as faces in the crowd and often behave accordingly. Personal contact between a teacher and each student at the beginning and end of a period, a lesson, a school day, a school year, and outside of the classroom will send the message that the teacher knows and cares about each person. Even eye contact at the beginning and during a lesson has a positive effect. Though this principle is not always possible to apply, allowing for independent and cooperative classwork makes this personal connecting more possible more of the time. Personal rapport between students and teacher and among students is the glue that holds the classroom together.

Group Behavior Is Founded Upon Individual Rapport

DOI: 10.4324/9781003230281-101

98

Outside of Business

It's cold outside or it's hot or windy. The teachers are tired and need to talk with each other. Nonetheless, the price paid for not being at recess (is there recess?) is too high. The benefits of not being with the students during some of this down time do not outweigh the costs. The sociology of the classroom demands that teachers have personal connections with students, especially certain ones. This relationship is in part forged by contact outside the necessarily more formal group setting in the classroom. Relationships are the classroom glue. At recess, a watchful eye is required so that conflicts do not escalate and spill back into the classroom. Teachers also interact with individuals and learn more about what is really going on in their minds and lives. When students know the teacher knows another side of them, they will be more motivated to function at a higher level academically, not to mention be more focused and in better control of themselves.

An example close to home is a teacher who spent the first part of a year staying in the school during morning (remember these?) and lunch recess, losing the class uncharacteristically and inexplicably. It dawned on this confused teacher that in past years, rapport had been the key to success and that rapport had been based in part upon umpiring games, playing with students, teaching them guitar, doing drama, and talking with them

DOI: 10.4324/9781003230281-102

outside the classroom. One month of returning to them at recess solved the problem. No need to have anyone write anything 100 times again. (Hmm...who *was* this teacher?)

The Glue of the Classroom

99

Punish Not All for the Sins of the Few

Positive classroom climate, focus, and order are a function of critical mass. A critically high number of the students must believe it to be in their best interest to be focused learners. The classic act of keeping everyone in for recess or proclamations such as "I'm very disappointed in this class" take away the incentive for the more appropriately behaving students to conform and reduce the percentage of students necessary for a classroom learning climate norm. To create a positive self-fulfilling prophecy for the entire class, reward the focused students and help the others individually.

Don't Make Goody-Goodies into Baddy-Baddies

DOI: 10.4324/9781003230281-103

100

When All Else Has Failed

Since all classrooms are socially dynamic, there are events that even the usually effective preventive measures do not deflect or prevent. "What to do now" is an on-the-spot question familiar to all teachers. When minor or major disruption occurs, a good rule or principle to follow is that of **least force** (see Glossary). The idea is to use the least force, or coercion, possible and proceed as the situation demands. For instance, when a student is disturbing a group discussion, the teacher intervention might include, in order, praising the positive behavior of the other students, to shifting to another response mode, to reminding the student positively, to proposing an after-class conference with the student, to moving the student within the group, and then to a seat in the room. Heated exchanges are to be avoided in the classroom "arena," as well as trips to the office. These trips cannot always be avoided in the case of violent or totally disrespectful behavior, of course. All of this is easier said than done but applying the "least force" principle is generally a wise decision. Since "educational reform" and professional renewal is a daily job, it pays the teacher to reflect in-depth upon the possible causes of the incident and ask what changes can be instituted to help prevent future incidents of the kind.

"The Fault Dear Brutus . . ."

DOI: 10.4324/9781003230281-104

Appendix

Figure A.1 Classroom Motivation Wheel

Classroom Motivation Wheel

Theoretical Factors, Their Definitions, and Practical Applications

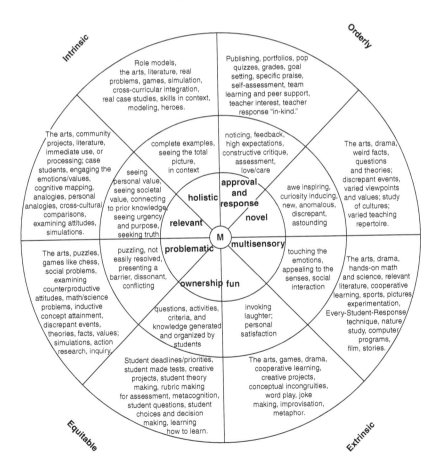

FIGURE A.1

A look at various forms of motivation and practical applications.

Figure A.2 Problem-Solving Action Research Flow Chart

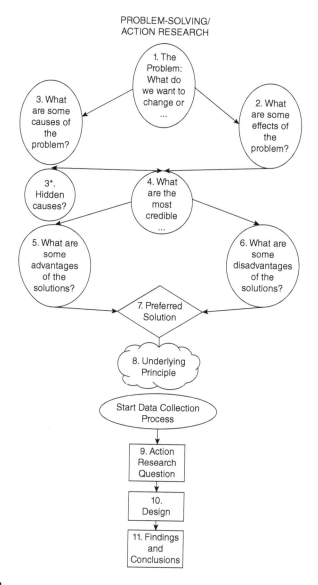

FIGURE A.2

A problem-solving flowchart particularly useful for professional development and university purposes.

Figure A.3 Problem-Solving Action Research Thinking

**PROBLEM-SOLVING/
ACTION RESEARCH THINKING**

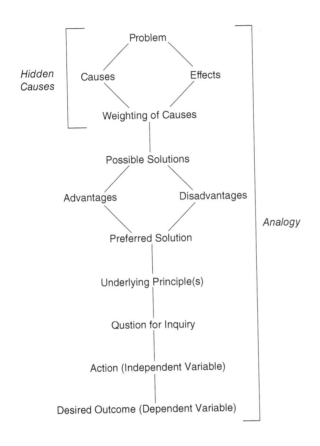

Original design by George Eley and Frank T. Lyman Jr.

FIGURE A.3

This cognitive path, or thinking heuristic, originated as a reflective tool to help beginning teachers solve classroom problems. The teachers were encouraged to go beyond the solution to a design for doing action research, thereby raising the attempted solution to the level of principle. Teachers discovered that by visualizing the steps, they could apply them in the middle of the classroom dynamic and solve problems "on the go." Some teachers introduced the thinking path to students and used the heuristic with them to solve problems relevant to the content, the classroom community, or the community at large. Advanced or older students are able to carry the thinking through to the action research steps. Modeling by the teacher makes this work.

Figure A.4 Problem-Solution Template A

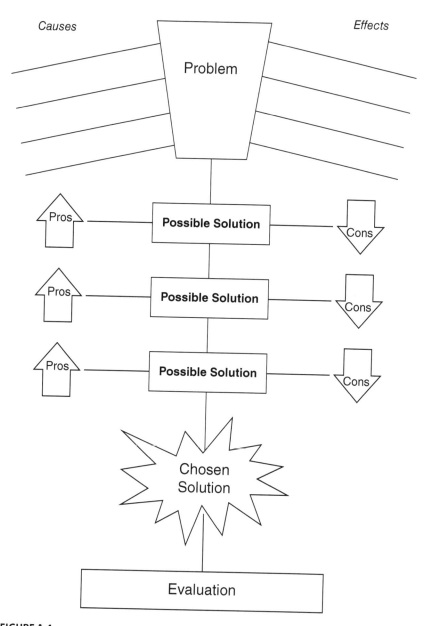

FIGURE A.4

Teachers or students do the analysis on their own in writing and can then polish their work cooperatively with a partner or group.

Figure A.5 Problem-Solution Template B

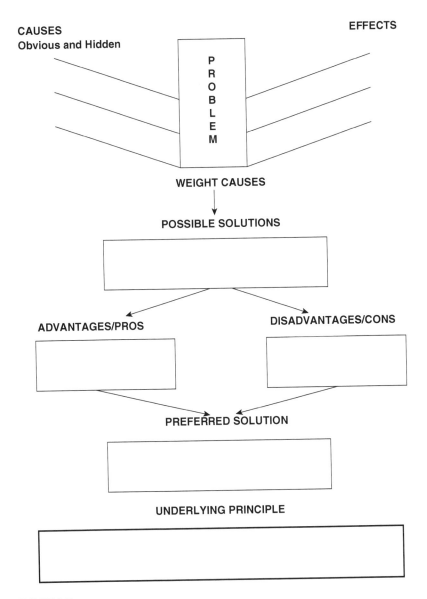

PROBLEM-SOLVING RESEARCH THINKING
DECISION-MAKING ORGANIZER

CAUSES
Obvious and Hidden

EFFECTS

P
R
O
B
L
E
M

WEIGHT CAUSES

POSSIBLE SOLUTIONS

ADVANTAGES/PROS

DISADVANTAGES/CONS

PREFERRED SOLUTION

UNDERLYING PRINCIPLE

FIGURE A.5
Alternate version. Teachers or students do the analysis on their own in writing and can
then polish their work cooperatively with a partner or group.

Figure A.6 Mapping Designs

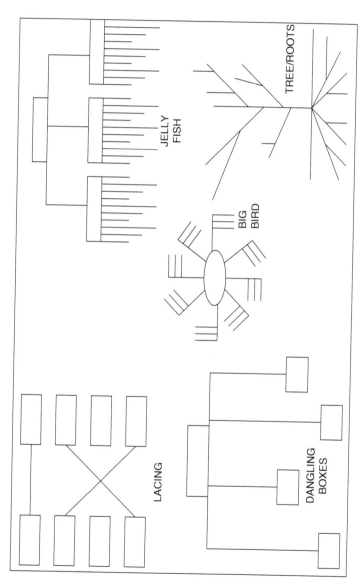

LACING

DANGLING
BOXES

BIG
BIRD

JELLY
FISH

TREE/ROOTS

FIGURE A.6
Five examples of visual maps.

Figure A.7 Concentric Circle ThinkLink

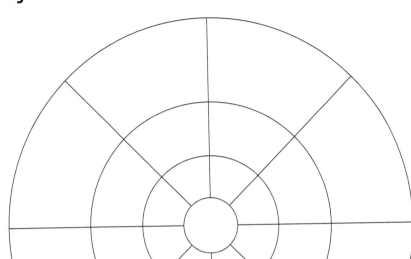

FIGURE A.7

This cognitive map, or visual organizer, shape is included because of its almost universal utility in connecting thought, especially in concept development through analogy. It can be used with a class to construct theory about any cause-and-effect analyzable phenomenon, and students can use it as a note-taking device or as a blueprint structure for composition.

Figure A.8 Class Theory of Think Time

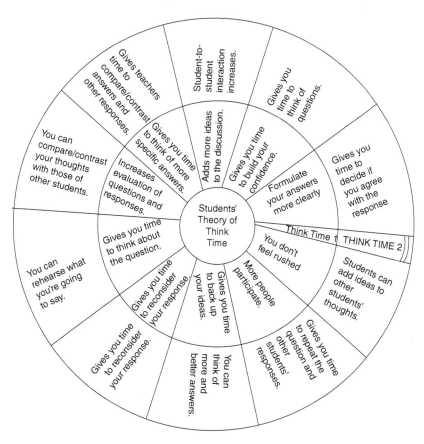

Donna Giarman's Fourth Grade Class

FIGURE A.8
The class theory of Think Time grade 5 illustrates student-constructed theory.

Figure A.9 Decision-Making Organizer

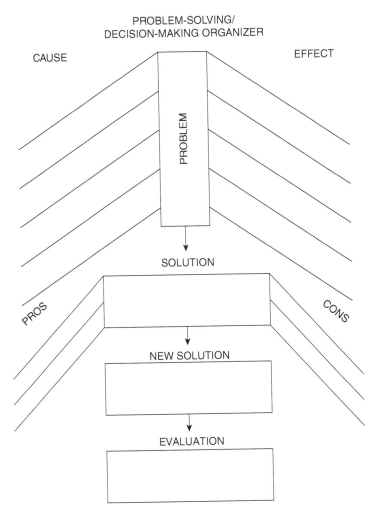

FIGURE A.9
This decision-making organizer helps students analyze the causes and effects of the problem and weigh pros and cons of solutions.

Figure A.10 Class Theory of Learning

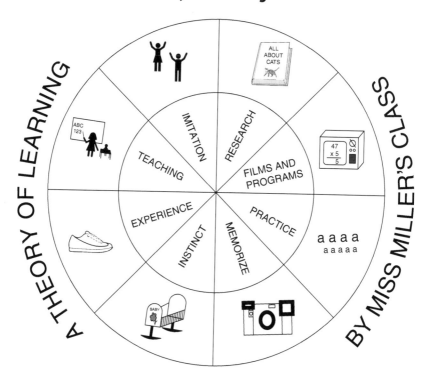

Kagan Publishing

FIGURE A.10
An example of Learning Theory Lab from Kim Miller's Class.

Figure A.11 ThinkTrix Science

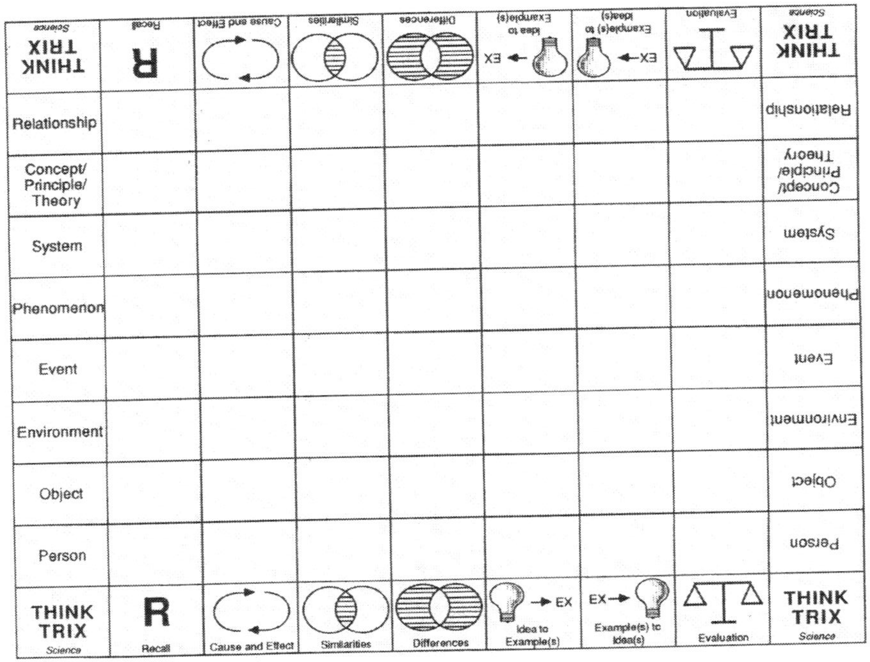

FIGURE A.11

This two-sided grid serves as a desk format for two or more students to work cooperatively to discuss science or any subject, creating, classifying, and answering questions. ThinkTrix grids can be designed for any content area by changing the departure points.

Figure A.12 ThinkTrix Social Studies

THINK TRIX Social Studies	Evaluation	EX→ Example(s) to Idea(s)	Idea to Example(s) EX	Differences	Similarities	Cause and Effect	R Recall
Relationship							
Problem/ Conflict							
Culture							
Concept/ Generalization/ Theory							
Story/ Extended Event							
Place							
Event/Fact							
Person							
THINK TRIX Social Studies	Evaluation	EX→ Example(s) to Idea(s)	Idea to Example(s) →EX	Differences	Similarities	Cause and Effect	R Recall
Relationship							
Problem/ Conflict							
Culture							
Concept/ Generalization/ Theory							
Story/ Extended Event							
Place							
Event/Fact							
Person							

FIGURE A.12

This two-sided grid serves as a desk format for two or more students to work cooperatively to discuss social studies or any subject, creating, classifying, and answering questions. ThinkTrix grids can be designed for any content area by changing the departure points.

Figure A.13 ThinkTrix Language Arts

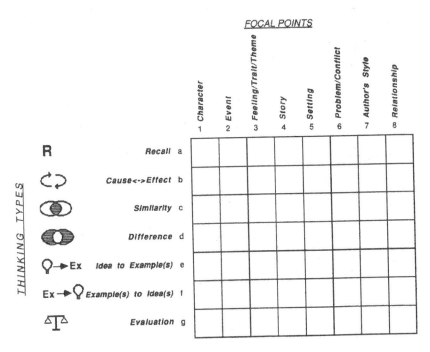

ThinkTrix
LITERATURE

The framework of thinking may be visualized as a matrix with one axis representing the focal points and the other axis representing the thinking types, or thought processes, involved. This framework is useful for reminding teachers and students of questions to ask and types of responses to make. The focal points below are examples of what is appropriate for reading/literature. They may be changed depending on content area or learning objective.

FIGURE A.13
This is an alternate version, shown here with a literature/language arts example.

Note

This ThinkTrix grid and the two-sided discussion grids (Figures A.11 and A.12) were designed by Belinda Miller and Sharon Vargo Olson

Figure A.14 The Reading Wheel

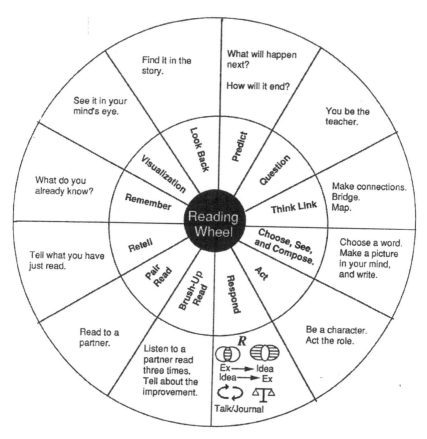

FIGURE A.14

The reading wheel was designed originally to give students options during reading group as they waited for other students to finish silent reading. The teacher set the arrows on individual activities they could engage in as they waited. This technique was dubbed "concentric options." Soon it became evident that the activities on the wheel were useful to remind the teacher of strategies for student response to the reading that could be employed at any time during the group discussion. The wheel was enlarged, enhanced through color and design, and displayed prominently.

Figure A.15 HOT! Handwriting

Hot!   Hot!   Hot!

Handwriting

Handsome (final drafts)

Okay (note taking)

Time-Saver (brainstorming, rough drafts)

FIGURE A.15
A reminder of when to focus on legible writing.

Figure A.16 Concept and Skill Development Planning Template

Essential Considerations for Putting It ALL TOGETHER

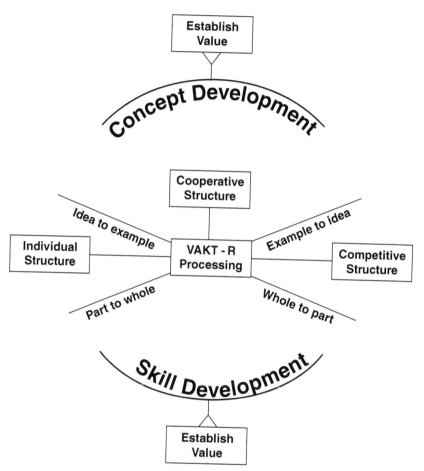

FIGURE A.16

This design has the function of reminding the teacher to consider which strategy to use when teaching a concept or a skill. Should the concept be taught from the specific to the general or the reverse? Should the skill be introduced by its parts or by presenting the whole first? What is the value of the concept or skill? Should the concept or skill be learned by the individual in a cooperative group or competitively?

Figure A.16a Planning Considerations

Ten Considerations for Planning

A Framework for Thinking About Instruction

1. What is the objective? (concept, skill, attitude)

2. How worthwhile is the objective (short- and long-term value)?

3. Do the students perceive the objective as worthwhile? (motivation level)

4. What are the roadblocks to students' meeting their objective? (barriers)

5. What do students already know? (prior knowledge)

6. How are the students going to learn? (how will they think?)

7. What examples will students need? (visual, auditory, tactile, relevant, etc.)

8. How will every student respond? (signals)

9. How will the teacher and students know what has been learned? (assessment)

10. How should the teacher prepare for the lesson? (rehearse)

FIGURE A.16a
Ten considerations for planning.

Figure A.17 The B Wheel

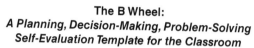

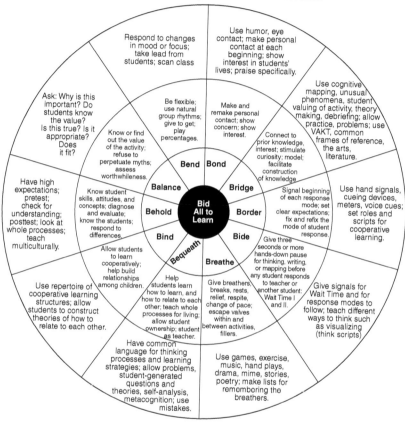

FIGURE A.17

This theory/practice template was designed collaboratively by teachers, student teachers, and interns to contain the most important instructional factors to be considered when planning or evaluating teaching. It was initially used as a guide for analysis of teaching/learning events. The purpose was to determine which factors on the wheel were present or missing in the success or failure of a particular event or classroom activity. It was never used as a checklist. As teachers and student teachers became familiar and conversant with the ten factors, they were encouraged to use it as a guide for lesson planning, as a kind of memory aid. The point here is that no matter how experienced or knowledgeable a teacher is, forgetting is the enemy. The common language the wheel provided enabled teachers to discuss the cause and effect of classroom dynamics more precisely and fluently. Some teachers enlarged the B Wheel to wall size and let students in on the "secret." It might be mentioned here that the wheel was helpful in job interviews. The candidate used a mental picture of the wheel to answer any question asked, particularly the classic, "Tell me about your classroom management." Some interviewers were dazzled.

Figure A.18 B Wheel Explanation

Planning, Decision-Making, Problem-Solving, and Self-Evaluation Through the "B's"

"Cogito Ergo Sum." I think therefore I am. Descartes sought to get down to what couldn't be doubted. Thoreau was fascinated with finding the hard bottom of Walden Pond. What is hard ground for a teacher? What are the essential causal elements of the ecology of the classroom? What is sine qua non?

These questions brought about the birth of the "B's." The first answer was "I love, therefore, I teach." Since love is the foundation, but never enough, another answer followed—"I wait, therefore I teach." When teachers and student teachers were presented with love and Wait Time as the two great commandments of teaching, they insisted on a third—structuring. So began the "B's": bond, bide, border. Teachers and student teachers were challenged to add irreducible key elements and then there were ten. Eleven wouldn't get on the wheel, so that has to be it.

The wheel design contains a common language and is an attempt to make crucial theoretical elements accessible to teachers at the point of decision-making. In the swirl of classroom events, remembering is often more the problem than is not knowing. The wheel suggests practice that is anchored to theory; it is a teacher's guide and conscience. Use it as a desk tool, enlarge it for the wall, place it where you can see it on your desk at home. If it has shortcomings, add or subtract or make a new one, try a "C" wheel. Cognitive tools such as the "B wheel" will make a positive difference in the classroom.

Appreciation goes to Joan Lunt, Bill Ferguson, Al McClain, Marjorie Rogers, Cathy Orlando, Monica Diaz, Leah Amato, and all the other University of Maryland College Park and Howard County, Maryland, student teachers, interns, and teachers who wouldn't stand for only love and Wait Time.

Figure A.19 Transactional Signals

THINK	PAIR	SHARE	ALL SHARE
DISAGREE	AGREE	NOT SURE	I KNOW THAT
IN MY MIND	IDEA	RECALL	SIMILAR
DIFFERENT	IDEA TO EXAMPLE	EXAMPLE TO IDEA	SELF HUG
GOOD RISK-TAKING	TYPE OF QUESTION	EVALUATION	CAUSE AND EFFECT
THOUGHT CONNECTION	PICTURE IT	MASK	WORK

FIGURE A.19

These are examples of hand cues that teacher and students can use to signal to each other response modes, states of mind, and mind actions. There are many more possibilities.

Epilogue

This book is for teachers. It is an attic of ideas in the sense that there is no order, and the ideas are not new. They are timeworn, though some are wrapped in unusual packages. The packages are techniques and strategies that teachers have invented and used with good results. The concepts and principles embedded in the packages are like gold within ore in that their value remains well beyond the specific activity suggested. These ideas can transfer to other levels, subject areas, and settings. When John Dewey said that theory is more practical than practice, this is probably what he meant. In his words, the teacher should have the power to "go on growing," not merely to know what to do on Monday. Many of the ideas and the related techniques, strategies, and attitudes in this book were hard-earned by teachers working their way through frustrating problems. Some are epiphanies that turned careers around; others led to adjustments in style or attitudes of less monumental proportions. Sometimes the idea preceded the strategy, other times the reverse. In all cases, they are representative of teachers learning in the classroom, with student, collegial, and sometimes university support. The items in the book are then the outcomes of teachers learning the craft, art, and science of teaching and should be viewed in that light, rather than as prescriptions to be followed. As in the rummaging in an attic, choose what interests you and bring it to the light of your day.

> To reflect is to look back over what has been done so as to extract the net meanings which are the capital stock for intelligent dealing with further experiences. It is the heart of intellectual organization and of the disciplined mind.
> —John Dewey, 1938

Postscript

The author of this book stands in awe of the authors/teachers of countless excellent books on teaching and learning. In no way does the author presume that the ideas/techniques/strategies and the embedded ideas in this book are the best or only aspects of teaching/learning worthy of inclusion. The attempt has been to put together in an accessible and theory/practice form some insights and related practices that have helped students at various developmental levels. One hopes the effort has been worthwhile for teachers—the truest hope for the advance of civilization.

Glossary

Biblioallusion—A reference to a familiar character, event, conflict, or theme from literature intended to clarify by analogy an event or a person's action. Often used in humor to gently suggest self-examination as in "Are you Tigger today?"

Big Idea—A transferable idea in the form of a concept (e.g., adaptation), a theme (freedom from fear), a principle (e.g., F = MA), or a process (e.g., writing). An idea that has the power to provide meaning and transfer, an activator of thought.

Borders—The marked or signaled intervals between segments of a lesson or between lessons. The clearer and the more accepted the signal associated with ending or beginning, the smoother the transitions will be.

Brush-Up Reading—A procedure wherein two students help each other by commenting on the improvement of the oral reading of the partner as the passage is read three times. This activity is known also as "Repeated Readings."

Cognitive Bends—The mismatch between a concept and a clarifying, fitting example occurring when the receiver of a communication is unable to connect a concept to a familiar example or an example to a known concept. The strained analogy is that of a deep diver suffering from decompression. This is avoidable when a teacher connects an idea to an example when addressing the class.

Cognitive Drift—A state of confusion wherein students and/or teachers are uncertain of what types of thinking are called for, remedied by the use of precise and mutually understood language.

Cognitive Mapping—The process of diagramming, or visually representing, thought. Known by numerous other names, including ThinkLinks, this "shaping" of thinking has enormous value for memory, cooperative thinking, pre- and posttesting, self-assessment, note taking, written composition, concept development, response to content, and use of the internet.

Cognitive Path—A series of steps, not necessarily always in the same order, that take a thinker to a solution, decision, conclusion, hypothesis, invention. The scientific process is an example.

Concentration Bubbles—The states of mind necessary for students in a classroom to focus on a task. These can be broken or "popped" by inappropriate seating arrangements, for example.

Conceptual Incongruity—A mismatch between prior understanding and a novel fact or phenomenon. Also known as a discrepant event, weird fact, anomaly, and by other labels, this incongruity can create the sense of awe, puzzlement, or wonder that engenders in students the need/drive to know more to fit the new learning into their prior knowledge schema.

Content Directions—In skill development, the movement from whole to part or part to whole, as in seeing whole models before learning skills or practicing skills without having had a sense of the whole product.

Every-Student-Response [ESR]—A moment in the classroom in which a maximum number of students are actively engaged in a learning experience that is relevant to them and worthwhile for their education. At its best, the learning experience would be differentiated for individual differences and engage each student's participation through several modalities. ESR is a goal, not an absolute that the teacher can reach every second.

Excerpt Publishing—Pieces of student work made public to serve as examples of excellence in written composition and poetry.

Focus—A term used in place of management to indicate the productive state of student awareness and responsiveness. This state is often primarily an effect of variables other than those commonly associated with classroom management.

Least Force Principle—The teacher's guiding principle to apply when disruption occurs in the classroom. For each stage of student noncompliance with decorum, the teacher uses the least forceful intervention possible.

Lesson Sag—A loss of student focus, often a result of students being unprepared to respond in a discussion or of the teacher "tunneling" in on or not regulating one student's response or nonresponse while the others are uninvolved.

Metacognition—Knowing how you know. This cognitive ability is one that places the learner/teacher in an aware state, able to think in a more conscious and strategic way.

Metering— Showing change by stages on a thermometer-similar gauge. Used visibly in a classroom to allow all students to estimate their attention to a task or the degree to which a task is completed. Sometimes referred to as a taskometer.

Metastrategics—The process by which teacher or student has a clear understanding of the thinking processes necessary for solving problems, making decisions, inquiring, and creating. This process requires envisioning a cognitive path.

Mind Actions (as coined by Sarah Lyman Kravits)—Thinking types reduced to the level where students know how they are thinking as they refer to them. As such, they are metacognitive aids that enable higher-level thinking as found in Bloom's Taxonomy. See "**thinking types**" and "**ThinkTrix.**"

Mind Hopping—The conscious movement of the mind from place to place, time to time, object to object, person to person, etc., thus enabling the thinker to access the past or present in order to find context for writing or discussion. This is controlled free association.

Poetic Classroom—A classroom designed to display the insightful, clever, and spontaneous words of the students, as well as illuminating thoughts from others.

Publishing Student Work—Displaying the best student achievement in various formats, including dramatic reading/acting, writing, and exhibits.

Rehearsal—The process of thinking through content before being required to respond. Wait Time and cooperative learning are vehicles for student rehearsal in the academic context.

Response-in-Kind—Teacher or student response that is direct and related to the content of the written or verbal message. This response is praise or criticism-free.

Rhythm—A concept that in the context of the classroom relates to how classroom events are flowing. Classroom rhythm can be manipulated by the teacher but not totally controlled, and in a "life of its own" moment, it can be ridden smoothly by the aware teacher.

Schema—Interconnecting patterns of knowledge formed in the mind, subject to change as knowledge increases or is challenged in some fashion.

Segment Theory—A set of principles related to moving from one activity to another or from one part of an activity to another. The classroom day is conceived as being divided into segments, and the smooth transitioning between them is essential for productive learning to occur within them. The teacher essentially provides an architecture for action within time.

SLSL—Student Learning Seconds Lost. The time wasted when students are not actively engaged in learning. Lack of Wait Time is a key culprit in increasing these unproductive seconds.

Substantive Sign Language (also known as **Transactional Signaling** as coined by Mary McKnight)—The signaling among class participants of mind actions or behaviors necessary for a task. Usually, hand signaling by students or teacher of mutually understood types of thinking.

Theory-Practice Templates—Teacher tools that contain both strategies and techniques for teaching/learning, as well as the theoretical basis for their use in the classroom. They can be used for planning, on-the-spot decision-making, and for evaluating. The "B Wheel" is an example of such a tool, and as do the others, it takes the burden off of the memory to decide what to do and why to do it.

ThinkLinks (as coined by Tom Bruner)—A student-friendly generic synonym for cognitive mapping, or for the other common labels such as visual organizers, graphic organizers, and mind mapping.

Thinking Types—Also known as mind actions, the seven fundamental actions of the mind are **recall, similarity, difference, cause and effect, example to idea, idea to example, and evaluation.** Though there is some overlap among the types, they are reduced to the point of accessibility for students and teachers and can clarify higher abstractions such as synthesis.

Think-Pair-Share—A multimode discussion technique in which all participants take time to think, sometimes then converse with a partner, and usually share responses with a larger group. A prompt from a teacher, group leader, or another student sets each stage of the process in motion. The technique is used worldwide at all levels of education and is designed to allow for maximum participation.

ThinkTrix (as coined by Tom Payne)—A reduced thinking taxonomy, or typology, containing seven basic actions of the mind, or thinking types, and sometimes placed in a grid, or matrix, format. Mutual understanding of the seven types allows teachers and students to communicate precisely regarding how their minds are functioning to answer questions, solve problems, and make decisions. Larger taxonomies such as Bloom's contain these seven types but are more general and less accessible to students and teachers within the classroom dynamic.

Transcendent Purpose—An objective or goal that seems of higher value than daily considerations, often in the context of helping others or creating something new for the common good. This can be seen as crucial for student development and focus.

Translating—The act of clarifying by stating a question or making a comment in two parallel ways, usually one way being less abstract than the other. Examples of this translating are the use of synonyms and the phrasing of questions using concrete words along with their more abstract counterparts. For instance, cause and effect with hypothesis.

Transprosition—A newly coined term that means the shaping of prose into a poetic form.

VAT— A symbol standing for a multimodality spelling test format in which the teacher cues the test takers through a series of modalities for each word of the test. The modes cued are hear it (listen), see it (visualize), say it, (subvocalize), beat it (break into syllables by tapping), write it (write the word), and drop it (place pencil down). This format for pretests has been found to improve spelling test results. VAT stands for visual, auditory, tactile spelling test model.

Voice of the Student—What the student says and thinks, an authentic expression of the learner's opinion, knowledge, and true intent.

Wait Time 1—The interval between the question being asked and the first response taken. To be effective on multiple variables, the think time should be at least three seconds, rarely more than ten unless the responders are writing.

Wait Time 1 and ½ (as coined by Chips Merkle)—A variation of Wait Time that allows thinking rehearsal time after partners have discussed together and before they are asked to share. Though not formally researched, this tactic is a valuable addition to Think-Pair-Share.

Wait Time 2—In a discussion, the time interval between the first response of a student and the next student response. Research has found strong effects on this variation, though it is harder to implement than Wait Time 1.